GRIEF AND GRACE

FACING THE FUTURE I DIDN'T CHOOSE

TIM TUCKER

This edition published in Great Britain in 2023 by The Message Trust.

First published in 2019.

The Message Trust
Lancaster House, Harper Road
Manchester, M22 4RG, UK

ISBN 978-1-7393073-1-8
eISBN 978-1-7393073-2-5

Cover design and typesetting: Simon Baker, Thirteen Creative

With love to Tony, Anne and Gareth. Words have never been sufficient to express my gratitude for welcoming me into your family. We shared in the loss of an irreplaceable treasure. I pray that His peace and love will continue to guide your steps every day.

To Team Tucker (Christina, Caleb, Samuel, Erin, Faith and the UK tribe), I love you with all my heart.

This book is dedicated to all readers who are facing a tragic event. I pray that my story will somehow encourage you in your time of crisis.

CONTENTS

FOREWORD

It is a great privilege and honour to write the foreword to this very moving and important book. I have known Tim since before Laura passed away and have stood with him in prayer and friendship during this season of his life.

I had to take my time when reading this book because I could identify with the grief that Tim expresses. I also lost my wife, not long before Laura passed away. As I read the contents of *Grief and Grace*, I often shed a tear or two as it helpfully enabled me to reflect on my own journey of grief and grace.

Indeed, Tim's story will help many people as they walk through their valley of the shadow of death. The apostle Paul writes in Philippians 1:12, 'now I want to you to know, brothers, that what has happened to me has really served to advance the gospel.' This principle is often replicated in scripture and certainly holds true in our lives as children of God.

The more I read the contents of this book, the more I appreciated the title, *Grief and Grace*. Tim has a fresh understanding of the multifaceted aspects of grace. This unique experience and revelation of grief and grace makes this a must-read for all people, not only those experiencing a season of grief.

I endorse and recommend that this book be distributed widely in every country around the world. It is my belief that every leader should have a copy on their desk/bookshelf as a resource through which they will better be able to support people facing grief and crises of many and varied kinds.

I recommend that you read Tim's story with an open heart to allow God to meet with you and bring healing and hope to your life.

May God bless you and keep you, cause his face to shine upon you, and bring you peace.

Pastor Theo Roman
Cape Town, South Africa

INTRODUCTION
THE GRIEF AND GRACE REFLECTION GUIDE

This edition of *Grief and Grace* includes a dedicated reflection guide written by Rev. Dave Meldrum.

Dave is an ordained Anglican priest originally from the UK. In 2010, he and his wife Bev moved to Cape Town, where Dave was Rector of a church until 2022. He is now exploring opportunities as a writer. He's a husband, father, movie buff, reader and sports fan.

The reflection guide at the end of each chapter is there to help you apply Tim's story to your own life and experiences. You can engage with it either by yourself, together with a trusted friend, or as part of a group. At times you may be encouraged to write/draw/create something pertaining to the part of the book you're reading; this might come easily to some but be a bit scary for others! While that's natural or understandable, we nevertheless encourage you to give it a go. It's not about producing something to show others, but rather aiding our own reflection by discovering a different way to express something that is true about ourselves. It's entirely your decision if you want to share it with anyone else, but there's no obligation or pressure to do so. In addition, there's a series of videos where Tim discusses the themes of each chapter on griefandgrace.org plus some extra resources for you to browse on that site. Use these for an even deeper dive into the themes.

DEAR READER...

This book is the story of the most traumatic six months in my life, from June to December 2016. I faced the unimaginable heartache of losing my wife, Laura. She was first hospitalised for five days late in June. After seeming to recover from a fairly inexplicable illness, and with no idea that her life was in danger, we went on holiday with my brother and his family in August. On the second day of the holiday she suffered what we were to discover was a brain aneurysm. Under the advice of the doctors, I gave permission for her life support machine to be switched off the following day – 18th August, 2016.

I've always kept a journal. From August to December 2016, during this period of deep sadness and confusion, I journaled voraciously. It was my means to process what had happened to me. My journal was at times raw as I wrestled with God over what had happened, and at other times reflective. Writing was part of my healing.

In 2017 I first began to realise that my story might be able to help other people who face unexpected and uninvited change in their life. I began to have opportunities to share publicly about what had happened to my family. It wasn't easy, but the feeling that my story could serve a greater purpose was a comforting thought. A number of people suggested I should turn my story into a book. I also felt a deeper call from God that I should do this. So, in 2018 I revisited and typed up all the journal entries. I identified themes and grouped them together... and this book is the outcome of that process.

What follows on these pages is not intended to be anything other than an account of what happened to me. It is not intended to be a manual or guide to handling grief or loss. Yet I do hope it will help bring courage and faith to those who face seemingly insurmountable challenges.

The book contains a number of my journal entries. These have not been included chronologically but rather in relation to the particular theme of the chapter. The dates are included for anyone interested in tracking where a journal entry fits within the timeframe of those few months. The journal entries are direct quotes with very little editing. The intention is purely to provide a link for you to the raw and immediate emotion/challenge/process that I was going through during my crisis period.

My journal also records poems, Bible verses, quotes and songs that spoke to me during that period. Many of those are recorded in this book. Some were sent by friends and family, while others I stumbled across in my own reading. They provided glimpses of grace, cracks of light in the darkness, and reminders that I was not the first, nor the last, to journey through the valley of the shadow of death.

DEAR READER...

Writing this story has been another key step in the process of my facing the future I didn't choose. It has helped in my healing process and my prayer is that some features of my story will resonate with your soul and bring you hope for healing in your personal story.

To help you in your own journey through grief and loss, this new edition of Grief and Grace includes a reflection guide. I trust you find it helpful. I have been humbled by the feedback I've received from Grief and Grace since the first edition was released. Please feel free to reach out to me through the Grief and Grace website: griefandgrace.org.

Tim

REFLECTION: DEAR READER...

What challenges currently seem insurmountable?

What experiences of loss and grief in your life are they related to?

What might courage and faith look like for you at this time?

CHAPTER ONE
THE COMMUTE

It was 29 June 2016. I left work at around 4.30pm.

My journey home from work that day summed up much of what we had accomplished over the past two and a half years. Since moving back to Cape Town from Pretoria in December 2013, Laura and I had attempted to align our lifestyle with our values and calling. During my 30-minute commute my mind was full of symbols of hope, answered prayers and signposts to future expectations.

It was winter, but the weather had the aftertaste of what had been a balmy autumn... with Cape Town experiencing persistent drought conditions. I stood on Main Road in Woodstock, hailing one of the notorious minibus taxis. As we lived close to work, I generally used public transport, so Laura could have the car. She home-schooled our three children (Caleb, Samuel and Erin). I often joked that our home was simply one campus of a network of home-schoolers who daily rotated their children from house to house. The schedule was complex and the world of 'home-schooling-moms' was one I was happy to plead ignorance about.

I was CEO of The Message Trust. We had founded the South African branch of The Message in early 2014, and I was very satisfied with the progress we'd been making. Our staff base was growing. Our impact amongst at-risk youth in prisons and gangs was gaining traction. And our new base in Woodstock was an exciting step towards fulfilling our dream of having a 'Leadership and Enterprise Centre'. This would serve as our operational HQ from which we could reach out to young people from across the city.

I say '*our*' dream because, although Laura didn't have a formal role at The Message, she was integrally involved. Over the previous couple of years, we had worked together in forming the first Eden team. In partnership with our church, Jubilee Community Church, we had recruited, trained and mobilised a team of volunteers who had moved into Salt River as a missional community. This may not sound like much but, in the Cape Town context, this was a radical initiative. Salt River is an urban neighbourhood bordering the city bowl which carries the legacy of apartheid inequality. Although Salt River is now undergoing development and gentrification, it has historically been an underprivileged area, notorious for gang violence and substance abuse. However, it also has a reputation of being a close-knit community, with a vibrancy that is not often found in the suburbs.

Our Eden team was a cross-cultural mix of people from various backgrounds and life-stages. They shared two things in common. Firstly, a desire to go against the societal norms of upward mobility: they wanted their address to be synonymous with their calling. Secondly, they loved the people of Salt River and genuinely wanted to serve the community by being in close proximity to them. These were not 'do-gooders' who would run projects, hand out food, take photos for social media – and then depart as quickly as they came. Rather, they were committed to long-term change through forming meaningful relationships. Laura and I had the privilege of having the team meeting in our home during their formation period in 2014. We loved hanging out with them, having deep discussions, and grappling with the challenges of relocating into Salt River. Laura thrived in the relationships she formed with the team. It filled us with incredible joy as the team became established in Salt River during 2015.

I was thinking about this as the minibus taxi hustled its way through the streets of Salt River and entered the neighbouring suburb Observatory – or *Obz* as it's known by locals. Obz is an 'urban village' right on the outskirts of Cape Town's city bowl. It has a reputation for being a diverse, tolerant and artistic community. It is home to students, young professionals, many international visitors, and an established street population. We loved living in Obz. We enjoyed having everything within walking distance of our house, including our church. And we loved that Obz is South Africa in microcosm – with the beauty and challenges of this 'rainbow nation' all merged into a densely compacted arena.

I escaped the confines of the crammed taxi and started mazing my way through the streets of Obz. Every walk through Obz is an adventure for the senses. As I walked down Station Road, I bumped into some of the homeless people we'd been getting to know. I greeted Victoria who, the previous month, Laura had helped with asthma medication. On a previous occasion we'd taken her back to her family home in Elsies River. But she always ended up back on the streets. Victoria, and many others, are long-term residents of

Obz, whose life choices are caught in the complex realities of homeless people. Laura's approach was to ensure that each person she engaged with knew their dignity and worth in the eyes of God – even if we didn't have direct solutions to the problems they faced.

As I approached the subway which would take me under the railway track which slices through the heart of Obz, I bumped into another friend and we exchanged small talk. We had recently started a community group for Obz residents who attended Jubilee Church. One goal of the group was to see how we could make a difference in our neighbourhood. We'd be meeting at our house again later that evening, a highlight of our week.

As I exited the subway and climbed the steps that brought me to our own street, I had one of those moments in life that should not be taken for granted, a mixture of joy and contentment which overflowed into a prayer of thanks, 'God, you really are bringing everything together.'

I pressed the button to our sliding gate and strode up our few stairs to the front door. Our dogs were there to greet me... Dory and Spike – Dory panting and wagging, Spike yapping and scampering. Laura and the children weren't home, which surprised me but wasn't unusual. I was looking forward to telling them about my day and expressing the satisfaction and well-being I'd felt.

Then the phone rang. Laura's name came on the screen. But it was Caleb's voice. '*Dad, you need to come... Mom's collapsed, and she can't drive us home.*'

It was a phone call that changed everything. The herald of a new era... one that was unexpected and uninvited. *It summoned me into the future we didn't choose!*

REFLECTION: CHAPTER ONE

Identify a moment, experience or process that changed everything for you and diverted you into a future you didn't choose.

Take some time to remember any details about how things felt before your enforced change. Describe it, sense it, feel it, express it.

Write, draw, create something that describes how that experience of change felt at the time – being forced to leave behind what you know for something unknown.

CHAPTER TWO

OUR PERFECT DAY

'Grace doesn't depend on suffering to exist, but when there is suffering you will find grace in many facets and colours.'

PAUL YOUNG

Laura and the children were at a friend's house, another home-schooling family, when she had collapsed as they were preparing to drive home. The friends took Laura to the hospital and I borrowed our neighbour's car and met them there. When I got to the emergency room, Laura was still not aware of where she was or what had happened. They took her for some scans and she slowly seemed to come around. One doctor thought of discharging her. But they eventually admitted her, and she underwent a barrage of tests over the next few days. The six days in hospital were a scary time. But the doctors found nothing sinister and discharged her, recommending a minor operation on her sinuses before further tests. There were a couple of theories, but nothing concrete. She was experiencing sensitivity to light and intense headaches, but these were diagnosed as symptoms of chronic sinusitis, compounded by a previously unidentified broken nose from childhood. In the meantime, Laura's Mom, Anne, flew down from Kwa Zulu-Natal to help me manage the home and the kids, while providing love, care and moral support to Laura.

A couple of weeks later, Laura was back at the hospital for the minor sinus operation. Laura was not unaccustomed to hospitalisation. As a young child she had chronic life-threatening asthma. And I had many times held her hand while she was wheeled into the operating theatre. In fact, we were so used to it that, because of a so-called 'important' work meeting, I dropped Laura at the hospital and one of her best friends held her hand as she went into theatre this time. But I made sure I was back at the hospital for when she came out of theatre. I was relieved when she was wheeled into the ward. Laura had already come around. I sat with her. We were hopeful that this would make a huge difference in her health.

At first there seemed to be good progress. The following week was our sixteenth wedding anniversary. One of the best decisions we ever made was to get married on a public holiday, always guaranteeing a day off together. August 9th is Women's Day in South Africa, commemorating the resistance of South African women to apartheid. We went for breakfast together, took selfies in Cape Town's Company Gardens, and talked about the children, our life together, and the future. We were excited by the imminent arrival of my brother, Paul, and his wife Megan and the kids from the UK for the holiday we'd been planning with them for over a year.

Two days before they arrived, Laura's headaches and light-sensitivity returned with a vengeance. She was bed-ridden while I packed to get ready for the holiday. However, having had several checkups the previous week, Laura was confident that she would still be fine to go on the holiday and had, as always, bravely mustered up the courage for the journey. We reflected that it was *déjà vu*. Seven years previously, on our last family holiday with Paul and Megan, Laura was rushed into surgery two days before they arrived. Facing the long drive to Mozambique for that holiday, everyone else had gone ahead of us while Laura took an extra day to recover, before we could drive up to meet them before crossing the Mozambican border. So, we had a track record. Laura always overcame adversity with grace and a smile, often enduring pain and stubbornly determined not to spoil other people's fun. That was Laura!

Following a 24-hour delay to their flight, my brother's family finally arrived. Laura continued to rest while I completed our packing. We all slept one night at our house before an early departure on the Monday morning for our five-hour drive to our holiday destination. The drive was tough for Laura, but she faced it with the stoic resolve that it would be worth it in the end. And so, we arrived in George at the onset of the world-famous Garden Route, ate at the American-themed Spur restaurant that evening, and went to bed with the peace of mind that comes from anticipating a restful and fun-filled time with family at the coast.

Which the following day proved to be. Tuesday 16th August was a perfect day. It was heavenly. Just the tonic we needed after the previous weeks of Laura's sickness and uncertainty since that call came from Caleb. And we were blissfully unaware of the events that would transpire in less than 24 hours.

That morning we had awoken to the sound of waves crashing on the beach in the distance and, from the stillness, I sensed it was going to be a stunning winter's day. We'd given the master bedroom to Paul and Megan. We were in single beds with Erin on a mattress on the floor between us. As I left the room to go and make breakfast, I gave Laura a cuddle, simply glad that she had been able to make the journey and that we hadn't had to change our plans. We had been praying that our time by the coast with my brother and his family would bring some healing and relief to Laura, as well as some much-needed rest for me. As we sat on the balcony overlooking Victoria Bay, Laura was relieved to have made the trip and glad to be with the family.

The sun was shining and the sea was inviting us to come and play. We packed up the cars and drove the short drive to the beach. Victoria Bay is one of my favourite beaches in South Africa. A small cove tucked away just past the town of George, a picturesque stretch of the Garden Route, it provides an idyllic location for a day at the beach. The wintry sun shone through on our family.

We had a fun-filled day on the beach. Laura mostly sat and contentedly watched everyone's activity and captured the day beautifully through the lens of our camera. Given that it was winter, we didn't want to waste the sun-kissed moment. We swam in the sea, played games on the sand and ate our picnic. I'd packed Laura her leftover bacon and avocado salad from the Spur the evening before.

Laura and I then went for a short walk to the end of the promenade and sat watching the surf roll, break, and then re-form as it sauntered into the bay and lapped onto the beach. Watching surfers always reminded me of a not-yet-accomplished goal to be able to, one day, stand on a board and cruise with a wave. Laura would reminisce of childhood caravanning holidays that enabled her to spend long summer days swimming in the sea and playing on the beach. She loved the ocean.

We then strolled back towards the beach along the Victoria Bay promenade. Hand in hand we were returning to our children who were now the ones playing on the beach. The kids were thrilled to have their cousins with them. Samuel and Caleb were playing with Joe. We could see my teenage nieces, Ella and Rose, chilling in the sun. For a moment we panicked… where's Erin? Our youngest daughter, seven at the time, is vivacious, daring and, like her mommy, absolutely loves the beach. But we couldn't see her! When we'd gone for the stroll, she had been happily entertaining herself. All parents know of that stomach-churning feeling when, no matter how momentarily, you cannot locate one of your children. But then Laura burst out laughing. A head donning a bright red swimming cap emerged from a deep chasm in the sand – Erin having dug a tunnel that any miner would be proud of.

Then it was ice creams all round before heading back to our holiday house. We were able to sit outside in the evening while I cooked steak, sausage and chicken on the braai. The kids rolled into bed and the parents had the deep satisfaction of a day well spent. Our perfect day. God's gift. Laura's perfect *last* day.

A few weeks later I wrote about this day in my journal:

6 September 2016

Three weeks since our perfect day

Completely oblivious to all that would follow. That my world would go from multi-colour to grey. That my future would cloud over and everything that seemed certain would be stricken to the core.

I thank God for how oblivious we were – how oblivious she seemed to be, to all that would come.

Time cuddling in bed
Full cooked breakfast
Sunshine day on the beach
Watching the children in the water
Her special packed lunch
Feeling the day was going so slowly
Walking and talking.
Looking for Erin on the sand but she's in a deep hole...

Typical Erin.
Playing Frisbee... making each moment count
Having a braai – wors, chicken and steak
Kids to bed... relaxing, chatting.
Our perfect last day.

REFLECTION: CHAPTER TWO

Tim describes recalling his 'perfect day' with Laura with thankfulness. This is a willful and defiant act of preventing profound loss from robbing us of the good that we enjoyed before.

Look back to the details you described at the end of the previous chapter, before your experience of loss/grief, and describe those things you are thankful for.

CHAPTER THREE

MIRACLES BUT NOT *THE* MIRACLE

> Yahweh, Yahweh / Always pain before a child is born
> Yahweh, Yahweh / Still, I'm waiting for the dawn…
>
> Take this heart / Take this heart
> Take this heart / And make it break
>
> BONO, U2

I've heard it said that, in a moment of great crisis, time slows down. And, similarly, when facing extreme danger and abject fear, one's senses become acutely aware of every detail. That was my experience of the 24-hour period that began at just after 10am on 17th August, the morning after our perfect day on the beach. It was my *day of days* which would culminate in me giving the instruction to switch off Laura's life support machine at just after 8am on the 18th August 2016. It was a 24-hour period that changed my life forever. And it was the most 'real' experience of my life, deeply engaging my mind, emotions and spirit. Quite clearly, this was the biggest crisis I'd ever faced. It was the moment when my worst fear became my harshest reality. My wife slipped out of this world right in front of my eyes. I was powerless to intervene and unable to change the outcome.

PRAYING FOR A MIRACLE

We awoke on 17 August with the contented holiday feeling that comes from having experienced a perfect day on the beach with those dearest to you. Our anticipation was that we would merely press 'repeat'.

I went through to the kitchen to make fried eggs on toast for everyone. We always felt that some form of cooked breakfast on holiday is non-negotiable. It makes the day begin on a different note when compared to the normality of porridge and our typical daily routine at home. But cooking breakfast for 10 people took time. So, it was one fried egg for everyone – except for Laura. Laura got two eggs that morning. Favouritism? Absolutely!

After breakfast I went to the games room with the kids to play some table tennis. Laura donned her sunglasses and went to sit on the balcony. The sunglasses had become a permanent feature for Laura over the last few weeks, even though it was the middle of winter. She wore them inside and out to counteract the sensitivity to light that she had recently been experiencing. We didn't know, at the time, that this was a warning sign of what was still to transpire.

While I was playing table tennis with the boys, she spent time with Megan and our eldest niece, Ella, identifying birds. When I joined them on the balcony, they were excited to tell me that they had spotted a Knysna Loerie[1] flitting around in the bush. Spotting such a beautiful and distinctive bird had certainly sparked enthusiasm for the day ahead, particularly as it is one that our family visiting from overseas would not commonly see in Birmingham! I was pleased to hear a lightness in her voice, an indication of the joy that being by the coast brought her. As ever, she was impatient that we get to the beach. The ocean refreshed her soul.

My journal entry on 31 August continues the events of that morning:

> *31 August 2016*
>
> *Our plan was to go to the beach again and seek to replicate the perfect day we'd had on our first day of holiday. Paul and I went to the shops to get things for lunch. When we got back, Laura's attack had just started and Megan was bringing her a damp cloth... my life was now changing forever... but I still had no idea that it would happen. I went in to Laura and asked Paul to go and find out where the nearest hospital was. Laura's temperature was spiking, and the wet cloths were turning warm immediately they were placed on her forehead. She passed out briefly and then came around. We both thought it was a repeat of the previous incident [her previous hospitalisation described in chapter 2]. I assured her everything would be fine... we'd now called for an ambulance. She was getting irritated by a lawnmower in the background – or the noise of the kids who were playing. She didn't want me to leave her... she cried out to the Lord in between*

1 The bird depicted on the front cover.

her cries of pain. 'When are they coming' she kept asking. She knew she needed the hospital. She couldn't cope with me stroking her head… I knelt by the bed and held her hand. She vomited… another sign we thought that it was the same as last time… but we both realised it was serious. We cried out to God.

The ambulance would be 30 more minutes. Bravely, Laura said I should take her [to the hospital]. She managed to sit up and Paul and I carried her to the car. She slouched on the back seat – still conscious. I followed someone to the hospital. 'How much further' she kept asking. My poor Laura. I tried to reassure her… it couldn't be far… this is a small place.

We pulled up at emergency. The ambulance was there, and the ambulance guy helped me get her into a wheelchair. She was a bit disorientated… but even when we got into the emergency room, she still managed to lift herself onto the bed. Then as they put the IV line in, she cried out in pain, and to the Lord – then was unconscious.

I didn't know it… but I'd lost her and soon she'd be in heaven. I can't remember if at that point I told her how much I loved her. But I do know she'll be glad I was at her side – she always wanted me, more than anyone else, at her side. And I was holding her hand and praying that God would spare her.

I was relieved to have got Laura to the hospital, although I was somewhat disorientated. They asked me to wait outside the emergency room, then called me to reception to fill in some paperwork. I gave a brief history of the past few weeks and that she had experienced an episode previously. I told the receptionist that the doctors had not thought it too serious but were still unsure of the root cause.

I then went to wait in the corridor. Those were strange moments. I wasn't sure what to do with myself. So, I just waited. A doctor eventually came to me and said that they needed to do a scan to see what was going on inside Laura's brain. She was still unconscious, and they weren't sure of the cause. He brought me through to her and opened her eyelids for me to see her eyes. Her pupils were severely dilated. An image that still haunts me.

Having gained my consent, they wheeled Laura through on a gurney into the X-ray room, while I remained on a bench outside. It was at that moment that everything changed. I think their intention was to do an MRI. But, as I was to find out later, Laura went into cardiac arrest. The next thing I saw was her being wheeled back at full speed to the emergency room. Although no one was communicating with me, I could tell that the mood of the doctors and nursing staff had altered. People were on high alert, running to and fro. One particular nurse passed me multiple times and I could tell she was trying to avoid catching my eye.

Eventually, a doctor came to see me. A kind and softly spoken man. I used to enjoy watching hospital dramas on TV but not anymore as it was like one of those scenes that are frequently repeated in a series like *House* or *Casualty*. 'The news isn't good'... 'do you have a friend or relative who can come and be with you'... and so on. For the first time he used the word 'aneurysm' which prompted a recollection in the recesses of my mind of that being some kind of internal time-bomb that can be triggered at any time.

The doctor was hoping to stabilise Laura enough to be able to airlift her back to Cape Town where a specialist brain surgeon would be able to operate. But he was preparing me for the worst. They moved her to the High Care ward in the hope that she would respond to treatment and stabilise sufficiently to cope with being transported.

I phoned my brother and asked him to come to the hospital. I also communicated with some friends and family. We mobilised prayer and trusted for a miracle. But as the day went on, the doctors lost any sense of optimism and admitted that we were now in the territory of *requiring* a miracle. The miracle didn't happen. By 9am on 18 August, my wife's body remained – but Laura was no longer inhabiting that frame.

She was no longer in this world. As Angus Buchan would say to me a few days later, she wasn't dead but had changed address – meaning she was in heaven and more alive than ever. Many people would say to me in the weeks that followed that they couldn't believe Laura was gone. But I had seen her depart this world, watched her take her last breath, and remained by the shell that was once my wife. She was gone.

MIRACLES

As the doctors followed their procedures and switched off her life-support machine, I remained by her bedside in a state of despair. I sent out a simple message to those closest to me: *we have lost an irreplaceable treasure.* I could sense shock waves reverberate as family and friends woke that day to face the news. Yet, even in that darkest place, I was also reflecting that God's grace had been with me throughout that desperately difficult 24-hour period. Even though we hadn't received the big miracle of Laura's life being spared, I could discern his presence with me through numerous 'smaller' miracles that demonstrated his love and grace to me beside that hospital bed.

My first entry in my journal written shortly after Laura died has two short sentences. The first simply states:

> *If Laura could have chosen how to spend her last day on Earth, it would have looked like Tuesday 16 August.*

I sincerely believe that our *perfect day* was a miraculous provision for us as a family. The children and I have often reflected on how amazing that day was. It felt perfectly orchestrated by God. And even more special because it was a day we shared with some of our favourite people on the planet – my brother and his family.

The journal entry continues with the second sentence as follows:

> *We didn't get our big miracle, but we've seen God in dozens of little miracles that have made this ordeal bearable and demonstrated his love and grace with us.*

Clearly the backdrop of these mini-miracles was against a series of traumatic events that nothing can prepare one to face. I was overwhelmed with grief. My mind oscillating between the enormity of what was happening, and the uncertainty of our future. A pervasive thought was, 'How will the children get through this?'

While everything was unfolding at the hospital on 17 August, the day had carried on as normal for the children. They played with their cousins and were oblivious to what was happening just a few kilometres away. Yes, Mommy was in hospital. But that had happened before, and they were not overly concerned. In childlike fashion, they got caught up in the things they were doing, and my sister-in-law kept them busy and active. Once evening came, the nursing staff on the high-care ward advised me to go home and try and get some sleep. Again, like an episode from a TV drama, they promised to phone me if there was any change in Laura's condition. She was now on a life-support machine and they explained it would just be a matter of time before her organs would show signs of failing. At that point, they would call me. I also realised it was important to see the children and explain to them what was happening. I wanted them to hear it from me firsthand. Once home, I gathered the children in the bedroom and shared with them that their mommy was critically ill. We wept together. And they asked, 'is Mommy going to die?' They told me later that they could see the truth in my face without me having to say the words. We prayed together and then all tried to get some sleep.

My phone rang at around 2am. Laura was showing signs of serious deterioration. They recommended I come so I could spend the last few hours with her. Once at the hospital, the nursing staff explained to me what would happen over the next few hours – until the point of the doctor coming on shift in the morning. They recommended turning off the life-support machine sooner rather than later, because then they could remove all the pipes and pumps keeping her alive, allowing me to spend some final moments with her as she breathed her last. I knew Laura would want it this way. It would give her a dignified departure from this life with me by her side – holding her hand. So, I had six hours left. And in the eerie peace and quiet of the high care ward, I had my final moments with Laura.

Unknown to me at the time, friends around the world were praying for us. I heard of some who had spent the whole night awake in prayer. Most had no idea of the seriousness of the situation. But I count it a miracle to be the recipient of so much love and care from people around the world.

As I reflected, both by Laura's hospital bed in the small hours of the night, and in the days that followed, I could begin to discern many mini-miracles that could be juxtaposed with the agony of my grief. The coexistence of *grief and grace* became part of my story during the course of that night.

Some might feel that the heartbreak was compounded because it happened on holiday. Surely holidays are meant to be a time of fun and joy? However, I came to believe that this was the first evidence of grace in our story. At that stage I travelled a lot. Imagine if this had happened to Laura while I was away from home. A few weeks before, I'd been in the UK... and a few weeks after I was due to be in the USA. It was a gift of grace that I was present and able to be by her side. Being on holiday enabled that to happen in a unique way. Additionally, we were on holiday with my brother and his family. When the doctor asked, 'do you have someone who can come and sit with you?', I could answer, 'yes, my brother is close by'. I wouldn't like to calculate the odds of that happening when we live over 6000 miles apart and only see each other every couple of years. We had a particularly special moment together at about 5:30 in the morning just before Laura passed away. I'd been alone at the hospital for about 3 hours, and then Paul came back to join me. We took a short walk to grab a coffee and prepare for the final stages. Just being with my elder brother at that point gave me courage for the journey ahead.

As we chatted over coffee, we were talking about how incredible the hospital staff had been. One of the nurses was particularly compassionate and considerate. She coached me through each aspect of the worst night of my life. She even prayed with us and encouraged me deeply. The hospital also arranged for the chaplain to come and sit with me. An Afrikaans pastor came and sat by my side. He prayed with me and, through my own teary vision, I saw tears rolling down his cheeks. I don't think I've ever experienced that level of empathy before. It felt like an angelic visitation. Someone who doesn't know me from Adam, and will probably never meet me again, reached into my heart and helped comfort my pain.

And somehow, being in the small town of George and away from 'normal life' gave our family a sanctuary to help us survive those initial days. Miraculously, within 36 hours of Laura's passing, all our close family had gathered from around the world. As each person arrived there were fresh tears as the enormity of the events continued to dawn upon us. There are numerous stories of what seems divine intervention that enabled this to happen. For example, on the day of Laura's attack, my parents were heading to Germany for my cousin's wedding. They took the call about Laura's illness while at the airport and decided they had to turn back home and await further news. By the next morning they were on a flight to South Africa.

As the family gathered at Carmel Guest Farm (where we'd been staying for the holiday), there were enough rooms for everyone to stay. Some close friends drove from Cape Town and we held an intimate funeral in George as that seemed simpler than transporting Laura's body back to Cape Town. A full memorial could happen later.

The day after Laura passed away, we all went back down to Victoria Bay. Many of us needed solitude and went to different parts of the beach but were comforted to know that we were all in sight of one another – all facing the same challenge of life without Laura. The children played with their cousins who were proving to be a healthy distraction. I walked and wept and considered what it was going to be like to return to Cape Town.

Now I had to face the future and just as that *day of days* had felt like an eternity, so my life would slow down with each moment feeling like a battle to survive. I had entered the valley of the shadow of death… and my journey of grief and grace was just beginning.

> *24 August 2016*
>
> *One week ago, my precious Laura had her attack that led to her death. As I carried her to the car and drove her to the hospital, I had no idea it would be my final moments with her. I knew it was serious and I was scared. I can't remember my final words to her. I think it was that we were nearly at the hospital and she'd soon be OK. I wish I had said more… although I know she knew that I loved her.*

We had cried out to God at the house... it was her natural response when in pain. She didn't want me to leave her side. I was able to try and care for her although I felt so useless. I couldn't stroke her head or her hair because of the pain. I said everything would be OK as I gave her wet cloth after wet cloth. She kept apologising – my Lau – that's what she did... always thinking of others. She would be devastated at my grief.

People say they can't believe she's gone... but I watched my precious Laura slip away into God's presence. She is gone and she's at peace. I am here, and God will help me work through this tragedy for he who made Laura and I one, will now heal my wound over time. But, for now, I am not whole. I have lost the one who completed me.

27 August 2016

Today was the memorial service. I'm thankful for how it went – a huge tribute to Laura – her life and her legacy. People from all sections of her life were there... hundreds of people all sharing in the grief of losing lovely Laura.

What I'm finding hard is not having Laura to talk to about how it went. I've lost my most trusted confidante... I have no one to debrief with. But I am trying to talk openly to people – to share my feelings and be transparent as I seek to process what I'm going through.

> *The children were so brave. I need to come to terms with the fact that I am now a single parent... something I've never considered. Wow – that's a reality to face.*

REFLECTION: CHAPTER THREE

In some ways looking for 'big miracles' is easy; not that the miracles themselves are easily achieved, but they are easier to identify and define. The 'smaller miracles' that Tim describes may be harder to define, getting lost in the search for something bigger.

Where have you looked for larger miracles, while potentially overlooking the smaller miracles around at the time? Try to identify and describe some of those smaller miracles which you may have missed. How might identifying these 'smaller miracles' help you understand the coexistence of grief and grace?

Tim talks about trying to transparently share with others about his feelings and the process of grief. This is not easy. What might stop us from doing this? What can help us to share more easily? Try to describe aspects of this for yourself.

When we find ourselves in a moment of crisis it is hard to start doing something that is novel and unfamiliar to us. It's almost as if we need to build up muscles to become accustomed to these new things during more 'normal' times, so that when a crisis does arise, those 'muscles' are geared up for the challenge.

How might you go about building up your 'muscles of thankfulness' in more normal times, to benefit your life both in the shorter term and to better equip you for the difficult times?

CHAPTER FOUR

SURVIVAL IN THE VALLEY

> Even when the way goes through
> Death Valley,
> I'm not afraid
> when you walk at my side.
>
> PSALM 23:4, MSG

9 October 2016

A touch of self-pity,
Am I allowed that,
every now and again?
Lord, strengthen me,
but let me be,
sad,
and a little lost,

> *For though I am not alone,*
> *I am lonely.*

UNEXPECTED AND UNEXPLAINABLE

I deliberately plunged you into my story in the opening three chapters. My intention was to enable you to feel some of the shock waves of my *day of days* and the events that surrounded it. The life I was expecting to live was permanently altered through what C.S. Lewis called an 'irreversible and irrevocable' event.

Now, almost 30 months on from what I've described, I feel it important to document my experience and trust that it will in some way be helpful to you. Perhaps it's appropriate to pause here and tell you why I have decided to record my story in this book.

A friend of mine once told me that to help understand something it's good to firstly explain the antithesis. So, let me tell you what this book is not: this book is *not* intended to be a manual for how to handle grief. It's not written to be a guidebook to help you navigate your own grief. I don't claim to have a certain number of critical steps that, should you follow them from A to Z, will help you recover from loss or trauma. No, I'd be lying if I claimed to have it all figured out. I'm not making promises to you that I can't fulfil.

Every journey through grief and loss is unique, so I do not want to be presumptuous about what others may or may not experience. This is simply my story, but I think the value of this book is perhaps twofold. Firstly, it simply recognises that bad things do happen to us in this life. It can happen to anyone at any time. No one is immune. One purpose of this book is simply acknowledging that fact. These cataclysmic events are both unexpected and unexplainable. They are *unexpected* in that they can happen at any moment and to any person. No matter how risk-averse we may be, we simply cannot mitigate for every eventuality. Stuff happens! It is part of being a human being on planet Earth. And these events are *unexplainable*. There is no simple answer to 'why' these things happen. As a theologian, that's a hard thing for me to admit. But this book is not meant to answer 'why' in some general or logical sense. I don't have the answers. I don't want to fall into the trap of stringing together clichés and slogans that trivialise suffering. Unexpected and unexplainable events *are* painful. I don't know anyone who puts out a welcome mat and invites suffering into their lives. But I also don't know anyone who has not suffered in some way. These events are experienced by countless people on a daily basis. Grief is a well-trodden path.

At the risk of steering us too far into melancholy and despair, the second reason for writing is to provide you with an account of how I *survived* the unexpected and unexplainable loss of my 38-year-old wife, and mother of our three children. I had no choice but to face the future that we didn't choose. This is my journey. In committing my experiences to print, my desire is that it will instil hope and courage to others for when they face the unexpected, unexplainable, irreversible and irrevocable events of life. Be it a loss of a loved one, retrenchment, divorce, or a deep betrayal, grief is an uninvited guest that can arrive at any point and make its home with you. Grief and trauma lead us into a valley that we would not have chosen to explore. This book lays bare some of my experience in the valley that I trust will resonate with your heart and mind and provide you with strength for your own journey of grief and grace. Although my experience and response are unique, I do believe there will be some common ground with people who are facing trauma. And perhaps in these places of identification, you will find some solace, healing, and direction through your own valley.

ON BEING TIM TUCKER

I am a unique individual and have processed my own grief as only Tim Tucker can. For that, I can make no apology. The events I've described, and the story that will continue, is unique to me. Some of it you will relate to, and some of it may well baffle you. However, I ask that you bear with me.

I didn't read many books in the aftermath of Laura's death. One book I did read was C.S. Lewis's *A Grief Observed*. It is an autobiographical record of his experience of losing his wife to cancer. It's raw and challenging as a seemingly reserved British academic bears his soul. But his experience was vastly different to mine. I remember being perplexed by some of his statements. It wasn't just because Lewis was writing in a different historical era or from within a culture that is not familiar to me that I struggled with some of what he wrote. Rather, it was because he was a unique person, facing his own individual challenges in a unique way. Perhaps that will be your experience as you read my account. If it angers or frustrates you, then please forgive me. If you need to skip parts, slam the book shut, weep with me, laugh at me, or shout obscenities to the heavens, then you have my permission to do so. Thankfully, you are not Tim Tucker and so have the liberty to process my story as you choose. I just hope and pray that it will ultimately be a healthy and helpful part of your journey.

My story is set against my own context. I was born in the UK to Ray and Christa Tucker. My dad is a Londoner and my mum German. My childhood was happy and protected. My parents were committed Christians, and I made a personal commitment to follow Jesus when I was a child. I was baptised when I was 9 years old, and also felt a desire to be a missionary while still young. We moved to the north-west of England when I was 11 years old. I went to a small Christian school and attended a vibrant church youth group. I left school at 16 and attended an engineering apprenticeship school. It was a rocky period for me as I sought to discover my identity and questioned whether I could *survive* as a Christian in an environment that was largely antagonistic. However, when I was 17, I nailed my colours to the mast, deciding to be a life-long follower of Jesus.

Although I had a fairly sheltered and privileged upbringing, there were a few experiences that made me aware that I was not immune to suffering. A defining period for me was when, at aged 19, I was diagnosed with Chronic Fatigue Syndrome. Over a three-year period, this left me severely debilitated, dependent on my family, and using a wheelchair whenever I left the house. I made a full recovery following much prayer and patience, but it was an experience that indelibly shaped who I am as I grappled with my identity and purpose in life. During the process of recovery, I felt called to serve in full-time Christian ministry. I resigned from the engineering company and started working for my local church as a youth worker. In 1998, I moved to South Africa. Ostensibly this was to be a two-year placement as a youth pastor at my Uncle's Presbyterian Church in Cape Town. Almost inevitably, I fell in love *with* Africa and I fell in love *in* Africa. Laura and I met in Cape Town in 1998. Our circle of friends occasionally overlapped. She was studying Occupational Therapy at the University of Cape Town. My flatmate was engaged to one of her classmates. We first hit it off at their engagement party. I asked for her phone number six months later at their wedding. We started dating in September 1999, were engaged by December and married the following August. We never seriously considered moving back to the UK. South Africa has been my adopted country ever since.

I've served in full-time Christian work for over 20 years. I have a doctorate in theology and still follow Jesus Christ as my hero and role model. My faith will permeate this book because that is the primary lens through which I responded to Laura's passing, and am processing my grief. I do believe in life after we depart this life, not as 'pie-in-the-sky-when-you-die', but as a reality which God desires each of us to experience as our ultimate purpose.

However, I do not believe you need to be a committed Christian to read and draw benefit from my story. In fact, if you are not a Christian, I hope that you will read on and engage with my story with an open mind and open heart. I do not see my faith as a crutch that enabled me to survive. But my experience of God was that he was right there with me in the valley. He walked beside me as my friend and ally. He shared in my grief and is big enough to cope with my questions, anger and jealousy. I will explore these aspects more fully in later chapters. But when I was beside Laura's hospital bed in the small hours of the morning on the 18th August

2016, my one prayer was, '*God, everything I've believed since childhood had better be true.*'

THE AFTERMATH

As I have re-read my journal, a word I frequently used in the early stages after Laura's death was the word *survive*. Laura and I had been great fans of the TV reality show, Survivor. In the early days of our marriage, Tuesday evenings were a sacrosanct time when we would sit in front of our tiny TV, and enter into the world of collusion, backstabbing and betrayal that enabled one contestant to survive and claim their $1 million prize. Ostensibly, Survivor was meant to be a battle against the elements of a deserted island or isolated and hostile environment. But it inevitably turned into a battle of personalities, wills and emotions as people pitted their wits against the twists and turns that emerged through unexpected events.

Similarly, my experience was that survival during the aftermath of Laura's death was a battle on many fronts. Some were obvious. Many unanticipated. However, unlike the game show, there was no tantalising external incentive or prize to help me conquer the battles I was facing. Rather, it was survival for survival's sake.

My context at the time required that I face certain realities. Upon returning to Cape Town from George, the first step was to organise the memorial service. We received incredible support from our church community, friends, and from family who flew to Cape Town from around the world. The children and I geared ourselves up for the memorial service. Caleb and Samuel were reluctant to be the centre of attention while Erin, by contrast, was looking forward to all the hugs and kisses she would get. The main thing we wanted was to honour Laura's life and to *survive*! My journal has brief reflections on the service:

> **27 August 2016**
>
> *Steve's[2] sermon was great. He quoted C.S. Lewis who spoke of the deeper the grief is proportional to the greater the experience of joy in life. That is so helpful – and relates to how I've been feeling about gratitude... being grateful to God for all he's done in my life through Lau... and I can rejoice in that. But it will take time for me to find new joy/happiness. I'll survive... but need patience and grace.*

> **28 August 2016**
>
> *Pastor Femi [a friend from Nigeria] said to me yesterday [at the memorial] that there is a special grace given for those who go through tragic situations. I do sense that. In the hospital, as the reality of Laura's condition set in – I just couldn't imagine how we would face this... how to cope with this level of pain. I couldn't comprehend how the children would survive.*
>
> *And yet, we are surviving in the midst of our pain, hurt, loss and grief. There is sufficient grace for each moment.*

2 Stephen van Rhyn is a friend and pastor of Jubilee Community Church

> *But I miss her so much. I want to talk to her about the people that came yesterday [to the memorial service]... how amazing it was to have people from around the world. I'd love to read the tributes with her. Discuss how awesome Siyoli and Meryl sang. I'd like to laugh about the funny things that happened... and cry about the sadness of it all. She would have been amazed at the generosity of everyone.*
>
> *'Lord you have trusted me to survive an immense loss. Please let your grace be sufficient for me and the children.'*

THE THINGS NO ONE TOLD ME

Beyond the memorial service, there were three massive and interconnected challenges that I needed to face. The first was what to do with the children. Laura had home-schooled our children. Caleb was now 13 and, in four months' time, was going to high school. Samuel and Erin were meant to remain in home-schooling, and they *wanted* to remain in home-schooling. The second challenge was not having any family members living in Cape Town. There was no one to 'step into the breach'. Thankfully, I have amazing parents and Laura's parents are equally phenomenal. They tag-teamed to stay with us for a few weeks after the memorial service. But it wasn't sustainable and having extra people in the house added its own pressure. I needed to reach a point of coping by myself. The third immediate challenge was work. My board had approved for me to have extended compassionate leave and I was overwhelmed by their support, as well as that of my colleagues, who stepped up to the plate. But did

I even want to return to work? Should I move back to the UK? Thankfully, I determined not to make any rash decisions while I was in survival mode. And, by way of a distraction, I also had the small matter of needing to submit my PhD thesis by November.

On top of these major issues, there was a list of what seemed to be unending tasks that required my attention. In fact, list-writing became a daily survival mechanism. The children joked that my memoirs should be called *The Life and Lists of Tim Tucker*.

I was talking recently to a friend who tragically lost his brother. His experience was similar to mine. In the immediate aftermath of the event, there was a ridiculous number of practical tasks that needed to be done. These are the things that no one can prepare you for and can crowd out any opportunity to grieve properly. Navigating a life-crisis can plunge you into a world of administrative, family and other responsibilities that you are ill-prepared for at a time when one's emotional reserves are at their lowest. My experience was that the seismic shift in my circumstances radically impacted my capacity. This is a reality of life in the valley.

Two journal entries help illustrate the nature of these challenges:

> **2 September 2016**
>
> *Another chapter in the 'experiences no one can prepare you for.' Had to collect Laura's ashes today. To be honest, if the kids hadn't got their heart set on sprinkling her ashes over the sea – I probably wouldn't have wanted to do it. Seeing my amazing wife reduced to dust… all that she was in body*

contained in such a small box... is somewhat disconcerting. I loved her body and it is gone – returned to dust and ashes. There is certainly a finality about it... but I'm not sure I'm ready for it in that sense. I'm holding on to the memories of all she was in soul, spirit and body, and it does sometimes feel like a dream. Surely this isn't the end for us... for Tim and Lau. I agree with Caleb that 4 is an unwholesome number. Yes, Laura told the kids she wanted her ashes spread over the sea, but she had in mind that she would have been old, and it would have been after a life well lived, having enjoyed our grandchildren and reflected on all that God has done. It would have been a celebration of her promotion to glory. But, although she has been promoted, the ashes represent what we have prematurely lost.

27 October 2016

I've been removing Laura's details from bank accounts etc. Every time is a mini-grief... a reminder as I delete her name from this world. The stark finality of it all. The death certificate a scroll that proclaims 'she is no more in this world' – she now owns nothing and has nothing – no rights, no voice to make decisions. Only history.

And yet I must remember that even though I delete things related to the bodily L that was my wife, she still lives on. She's in a place where she doesn't need a bank account, credit card or cell phone. The stuff that we acquire, only to leave behind, is a fleeting tie to this temporal world. And

> *every administrative task I undertake simply underscores our mortality and the futility of pursuing the stuff of this world.*
>
> *Laura is released from this stuff... and the cares and stress that goes with this life. And she has found true life. And that is more than a little consolation.*

GRACE

These, and other moments like them, were tough experiences.

The relationship with Laura's ashes was one of the strangest experiences of my life. Because the funeral and cremation had taken place in a rush, there was no way of acquiring and bringing back her ashes with us when we returned from George to Cape Town. So, I ended up having to collect the urn from a person I'd never met before, who had the unfortunate task of being the courier of Laura's ashes. I brought the urn home. It was in a 'gift bag' with the name of the undertakers stamped on the front. I stuffed the urn, still in the bag, into a cupboard by the bed. Our original plan was to have a small family service to spread the ashes over the ocean on Laura's birthday – a few weeks after the memorial service. Laura's parents were still staying with us and it seemed important to do it together. However, through a discussion with my counsellor, I realised I was applying too much pressure on myself and the family to do this. We weren't able or ready to cope with another emotional event! I suggested to my in-laws that we wait for another time. I saw the relief in their eyes as we were all trying to stage an event we weren't ready for. We realised that we needed to be kind to ourselves and allowed ourselves a gift of grace – and decided to wait. There was no need to rush. We eventually scattered Laura's ashes in July the following year. It was an intimate service which Laura's brother beautifully convened. We spread her ashes at Rocky Bay in KwaZulu Natal; a place which held special memories for Laura and the Simpson family.

One word I used in my journal was that I'd been *blind-sided*. The events had caught me unawares and unprepared. Perhaps one definition of grace should be that it gives us the strength to be resilient. I see now that resilience in the face of adversity was a gift of grace – perhaps the *special grace* that Pastor Femi had mentioned.

I wrote above about the three challenges I faced in the direct aftermath of Laura's passing. With the perspective of hindsight, I see that each challenge enabled me to experience the gracious gift of resilience. The children were a gift of grace. I *had* to care for them. They needed feeding, comforting, and keeping occupied. We started 'Daddy' schooling... which included media studies (going to the cinema), nature studies (going to the beach), and accounting (playing Monopoly). As mentioned, my parents and immediate family were amazing. But the time came when they had to return home. This forced me to pick up the reigns and carry the load. For me, busyness – even though I was exhausted – was a blessing. I note in my journal that *distraction* was critical. And this counted also for work. I took extended time off from my day-to-day leadership at The Message. However, after less than a two-month break, I needed to crack on with my PhD. I didn't want to defer it and have to face completing it at another time, particularly when I was so close to submission.

Therefore, the children spent some time with other friends who home-schooled (we called it friend-schooling), and I split my time between working at the office or at home, in order to complete my thesis. In some ways it was an empty exercise as I'd lost my passion for doing it. However, it was a gift of grace that I had something that could occupy my mind and provide a constructive distraction. I submitted my thesis in November. On time. A consequence of grace!

REFLECTION: CHAPTER FOUR

Tim says that the unexpected, cataclysmic events of life are unexplainable. What's your reaction to this? Are there explanations you find persuasive and convincing? What are the strengths and weaknesses of these explanations?

Tim describes three challenges: 1) what to do with the children, 2) not having the support of family members in Cape Town, and 3) related to his work.

How do you react to the idea that the challenges Tim described have enabled him to grow in the grace of resilience?

Does the grace of resilience produced through the challenges nullify any of the pain of the challenges; if the answer is 'No', how might it then change the way we see the challenges?

Tim talks about the 'things no one tells you about' that come in the wake of change and grief. Can you think of a change in your life – e.g. a relationship, a job, moving home - that brought with it things without any warning, and what nobody had told you to prepare for? Can you think of similar issues that might arise due to unwanted and sudden change?

CHAPTER FIVE
LIFE IN SLOW MOTION

> Bereavement is a universal and integral part of our experience of love. It follows marriage as normally as marriage follows courtship or as autumn follows summer. It is not a truncation of the process but one of its phases; not the interruption of the dance but the next figure.
>
> Sorrow, however, turns out to be not a state but a process.
>
> C.S. LEWIS

In March 2017, I sat chatting with some close friends. Danielle had been one of Laura's best friends and felt her loss deeply. She had been among the intimate group of friends and family that had come to George immediately upon hearing of Laura's death. And, since that time, she and her husband, David, had been a tremendous support to the kids and me, while also navigating her own grief.

We were in the garden having a good catch-up conversation while our children were inside occupying themselves. It was an important debriefing conversation. The children were now in their respective new schools and I was back at work full time. Seven months had passed. Yet, as I explained to them, it had felt like years of life had been lived in that relatively short space of time since we had said goodbye to Laura.

Time had taken on new significance for me. I became incredibly aware of it – my grief led me through an intense cognisance of the passing minutes, hours and days.

In 2006 I bought Laura a CD for Christmas by the artist David Gray. We were temporarily living out of suitcases in the UK during a seven-month fundraising and partnership development trip. So, our music collection was a bit limited (as these were the days before being able to stream music to your heart's content). Therefore, this album got played on repeat during our time in the UK, such that it didn't get much air-time once we returned to life in South Africa. However, the title track was indelibly imprinted on my mind, and helps describe my relationship with time while walking through deep grief. The track is called *Life in Slow Motion*.

> While I was watching you did a slow dissolve
> While I was watching you did a slow dissolve
> While I was watching you did a slow dissolve
>
> Did I imagine or do the walls have eyes
> Did I imagine they held us hypnotised
> Did I imagine or do the walls have eyes
>
> Life in slow motion somehow it don't feel real
> Life in slow motion somehow it don't feel real
> Life in slow motion somehow it don't feel real

LIFE IN SLOW MOTION

> Snowflakes are falling I'll catch them in my hands
> Snowflakes are falling I'll catch them in my hands
> Snowflakes are falling now you're my long lost friend

As with all the songs, poems or quotes I refer to in this book, it's not the entirety of the piece that describes my experience. Rather, it's an aspect or a glimpse into the struggle that helps illuminate a certain aspect of my grief. This song, for me, helps describe the challenge of *time* when facing deep loss. Life went into slow motion and, although watching Laura pass away was the most intensely real experience of my life (as described earlier), the following days, weeks and months took me to an unimagined world of learning to exist and live in slow motion. The snowflake metaphor that Gray uses is an apt description. Unlike heavy rain or driving hail, snowflakes flutter around in the wind and take an age to settle. They hypnotise children on cold wintry nights (sorry to my readers in Africa – hopefully you've seen snowflakes in the movies). My life was in slow motion, blowing in the breeze, taking an age to settle.

Initially I would count the days since Laura passed away. Then the weeks, particularly struggling on every Thursday. Then the 18th of every month became significant as an anniversary of her passing. It was the opposite of young lovers who note and celebrate the significant days that initiated their joyful courtship. In sharp contrast, it felt like, with the passing of every moment, all that we'd built up over 16 years of marriage was being unravelled.

My journal entries reflect both the nature of life in slow motion and some of my reflections on the challenges of time while I was walking slowly through the valley of the shadow of death.

> *7 September 2016*
>
> *Three weeks: seems like a lifetime has passed: feels like she should be a breath away.*
> *We're all waiting for her to walk back into our lives.*

> *18 September 2016*
>
> *And today was a painfully slow day – time ticked by so slowly… and I don't think inactivity helps me… I need to be careful of what may make me feel vulnerable and alone. Today I did.*

> *24 September 2016*
>
> *Haven't slept well…*
>
> *These 5 and a half weeks have felt like a lifetime – but time still moves forward – moving me away from the horror of losing Laura, away from the time we spent together and towards a future without her…*
>
> *'Time heals' they say. No doubt. But time also feels like an enemy because maybe I don't want to be healed yet… maybe*

I want to linger... to abide... to dwell further in the normal I had before a new normal arrives.

But time doesn't allow. And probably if it did, I would go mad.

But time is making me feel more distant from her and for now I want to resist that. I need to find ways to keep memories alive – even if I know I can't always trust my memories. I don't want to mythologise Laura or exaggerate what we had. But I want to recall, to celebrate and to relive special times... or, indeed, even ordinary moments.

Yet I'm also waking up thinking about the future... considering what may come, preparing for what time is leading me towards. Although I want to resist and cast my mind back – I guess it's part of what makes me human – or, more specifically, part of what makes me Tim. And part of being Tim is being in Christ, Lord of time who is leading me forward.

20 November 2016

I'm realising that there's a lot of time to fill – just day to day. At the moment, my PhD keeps me occupied. In some ways I'll be relieved when it's finished, but it's also been a companion for three years... filling quite a bit of time – when I really didn't need to fill time. But now, when I have time, I'm saying goodbye to this companion and wondering what

> *will replace it. Do I just fill the time with trivialities and entertainment? I guess there's a danger I'll fill it with work – once I'm back. Not that that's bad... but I'll need to be careful. Maybe when next year starts it'll be different because of school and a very full life/routine. But it's these early mornings and late nights... and some weekends – the time that was primarily our time together... that I'm realising is a fair portion of each day.*

I still note the 18th of every month, although not as I used to do. The pain is not as deep. It is more of an acknowledgement of the significance that each 18th held, a day that seems like an aeon ago. I'm writing this in December 2018. Two days ago, it was 28 months since Laura's passing. I imagine that, at some stage, this will change and these regular anniversaries of life in slow motion will change. In fact, as I look back upon those early days of life in slow motion, I realise now how much has changed.

W.W.L.D.

The initial struggle was to simply keep going. To get up, get dressed, prepare food, and face the various tasks of each day. I broke the days down into segments. Taking care of the kids' needs was the priority. Then undertaking various tasks that somehow suddenly felt important. Tasks that previously were lower on my list of priorities. My journal helps explain:

6 September 2016

I have this strange urge to complete unfinished tasks that I know Laura either wanted or things I wish I'd done for her. Whether in the garden or around the house – even doing the passports and Erin's hair... I think it's connected to wishing I'd done more to show her how much I love her... and/or it keeps me connected to her in some way. I want to please her. I want her to be proud of me. There was no greater joy than knowing I'd brought Laura pleasure... and I know she lived to please me.

The unfinished tasks included various home improvements, things we'd chatted about for years but never got around to finishing. Two new mottos helped govern what I would do each day. The first was, *living to make Laura proud...* I determined to live in such a way that honoured her memory and would have made her proud of me. The second was *What Would Laura Do (WWLD)*? I didn't get a wristband made like the WWJD (What Would Jesus Do) bracelets of the 1990s, but I did ask the question several times each day as I sought to navigate my new role and my new life.

1 October 2016

And yet I've found a new slogan to help motivate me on days like today: 'Living to make Laura proud' – and in a sense I've realised that I can still live for her as I have always done. And I've found some satisfaction in realising that Laura would be proud of me – getting to grips with things outside of my comfort zone. She'd be proud of me doing Erin's hair, chatting through 'stuff' with Caleb, making time for Sammy, managing the house, doing the memory garden and books etc. She would be proud that I completed the packing today – and that single thought is incredibly motivating. I knew her so well that I know she will be proud of me, she'd believe in me that I can do this – I can survive, and I can get through days like today.

But important tasks cannot fill every moment of every day. The downtime, the mundane times, were the most challenging. There was a void. I called it my sixth sense – the one that constantly reminded me that the world wasn't as it should be. And the sixth sense was like a trump card that could override all other senses, making an uninvited appearance at any time. A few weeks after the memorial service, the kids and I went away for a couple of weeks. A chance to be together, just the four of us. But I couldn't escape from my new sixth sense:

12 October 2016

I would describe my new disposition as having developed a sixth sense… the constant but not always cognitive sense that L is missing. It's always there – like oxygen, but there are times when the sense is more profound – a sharp pain, and there are other times when it's more like a dull ache. But it impacts each moment and also explains my weariness.

Today is one of the tough days.

We've had a couple of busy days culminating in going to Sun City yesterday. But today we have nothing planned (the kids need it) – but it's days like today that are the toughest – where the 6th Laura sense is acutest.

Just been on a walk on my own. I forced myself to do it as walking/being alone is so tough. I have been filling the days with activity and planning – but inevitably there are going to be gaps where I have to face the reality of Laura not being with me. And there's no escaping it. The finality of what happened 8 weeks ago causes deep hurt and pain that I simply can't always be distracted from.

19 October 2016

One thing I realised is the level of change in my life. I'm a changed man – living with this 6th sense. My circumstances and life have changed almost beyond recognition. My emotional life, my decision making, my capacity, my experience of joy, my desires etc. – all changed. 'Thanks, God, for the consistency of my faith.'

My experience of the sixth sense remains. However, it has become less dominant. It has become like an old injury that can unexpectedly flare up at any point when triggered by an event, experience, dream, memory, person or thought. The sixth sense was like a smog that had descended on me in those early months, engulfing all my other senses. The smog did lift, and I learned to breathe fresh air again. But when the sixth sense is triggered, the smog descends. I find that I firstly have to recognise it for what it is. Perhaps it's a form of post-traumatic stress. But, to me, it's the sixth sense and I have to once more navigate my way through it, knowing the smog will lift as it has done before. But, in the meantime, I need to be kind to myself. If tears come, they come. If not, don't feel guilty. Prayer and patience. Grief and grace. The smog will lift. It always does in the end.

MY THREE RULES

As I've already mentioned, a major challenge of life in slow motion was the inevitable times when I couldn't keep occupied. These were the times when loneliness was most intense. The challenge of keeping occupied is that it requires energy. But I was just so darned tired all the time. Grief is exhausting. The sixth sense sapped energy. Taking care of myself, the kids, doing what tasks I could, keeping abreast of what was happening at work and continuing my PhD – while not sleeping well – meant I was tired. And tiredness makes one vulnerable.

Laura and I had never been huge TV viewers. There were certain series we enjoyed. But we didn't have satellite television. So, one of the first things I did to fill the space in my life was to get DSTV installed with a link to a new TV in my bedroom. I'm a big sports fan. Ninety percent of my TV viewing was watching sport. It seemed a healthy distraction. However, I was aware of certain dangers. And, as a Christian desiring to live my life in a way that honours God, it was a vulnerable time for me.

Twelve weeks into life in slow motion, I wrote the following:

10 November 2016

I don't think I've written this, but I'm also committed to serving God in purity and to avoid every kind of evil. I need to take every thought captive – as my mind needs subjecting to Christ. I've decided to be really careful with alcohol – and not to have it in the house… I realise it could be easy to turn to alcohol during this time. I need to guard what I watch – nothing with sexual images etc. I want to remain faithful to God and Laura (I've actually been amazed how God has removed sexual desire – but I don't want to give it a doorway). And I want to be careful about spending time with women – particularly single women (who actually scare me half to death anyway). I'm completely committed to celibacy unless God calls me into marriage at a later stage in life. But if he doesn't, then I'm content. The 16 years I had with Laura were perfect and if that's God's gift to me, then I can be satisfied with that and content in him.

So, my three rules emerged to help me steer myself through this vulnerable time:

1. No alcohol. I was aware of how turning to drink could be a temptation during this lonely period – something I've seen have disastrous consequences for other people. Alcohol could also compromise me in other areas, so I knew I needed to keep myself in check.
2. Watch what I watch. I didn't watch anything rated above PG-13 and late at night I would only watch sport or news.

3. Avoid being alone with single women. There were places I didn't want my mind to go to and so it was easier for me just to have strict rules that I applied during those initial months.

Underlying these rules was both a desire to honour God, but also in relation to living for Laura. In respecting her memory.

GRACE

Although it didn't make it to my list of rules, a medium of grace for me was maintaining physical fitness. In 2017 I hit my straps with this as I rejuvenated a passion for running which I'd had in my twenties. With the family responsibilities, I couldn't carve out the time for long-distance running. Rather, I focused on distances between 5km and 10km. The weekly parkrun was a gift of grace. If you don't know about parkruns, then you are missing out! A global movement that provides a free timed 5km race every Saturday morning, it provided fresh motivation for me to keep fit. And the fact that it gave a timed result every week appealed to my competitive nature, inspiring me to attain new personal bests. I had a target to be able to run 5km in under 20 minutes – a target I attained in August 2017.

In the latter months of 2016, however, it was life in slow motion – which meant walking, rather than running. Since we launched The Message in 2014, we've had an annual fundraiser which is now called The Triple Challenge. It involves walking up all three of Cape Town's mountains in one day.[3] The event takes place in October and motivated me to get out of the house and spend time on the mountain. What was even more special is that we decided to do it as Team Tucker. We started a training regimen and got a few hikes under our belt. We loved being on the mountain together – another component of 'Daddy Schooling'. The day itself was a great event. It was good to be with people from The Message. The first mountain (aptly called Devil's Peak) was the toughest as the conditions were fairly grim and I had to coach and carry Erin some of the way. As the day went on, the weather improved to perfect hiking conditions. By the time we got to Lion's Head, Team Tucker strode to the summit and had a great catch-up conversation with one of my colleagues, Jess Longe, and her husband, Greg, along the way.

The sense of accomplishment was a means of grace. Overcoming the physical mountains served as a great metaphor for us on our walk through life in slow motion… our journey in the valley of the shadow of death. A little while later, we spent a couple of days with Laura's brother and his family in Pretoria. I wrote:

> *15 October 2016*
>
> *Today I took a long walk from Gareth and Michelle through to our old house [where Laura and I had lived when we were in Pretoria]. Walking, thinking, praying. Walking through a crisis… it reminded me of the role walking played as I*

3 Table Mountain, Devil's Peak, and Lion's Head are the three mountains that provide the panoramic backdrop to the city of Cape Town.

recovered from ME and conversed with God – walking down the valley in Broadbottom[4] or along The Mudd. I've noted before that walking was crucial for Laura and me in connecting together and making key decisions. We loved to walk places and were determined not to be just car dependent. But walking was not just an environmental or counter-cultural statement… it was a way of slowing things down, to reflect, to engage and to process. We did that throughout our relationship – wherever we lived. Now I need to walk with God… physically, metaphorically – so I can slow things down, think deeply, reflect and process in this phase of my journey.

Walking through crisis – again.
Keep on walking.
Just putting one foot in front of the other.
Sacred pauses.
Walking slowly through grief.

Three weeks after Laura's death, my good friends Alan and Jenny Smith sent me a poem. It might be a familiar poem to anyone who has experienced grief or loss. But it was new to me and a piece of art that takes on a far deeper significance when one is walking a similar road. Of everything people sent me, I found this poem the most helpful. It resonated with my experience, validated my processes, and enabled me to be kind to myself. It was a means of grace as I faced life in slow motion.

4 Broadbottom is a village just outside Manchester. I lived with a family who lived on The Mudd while I was recovering from having Chronic Fatigue Syndrome (ME).

Walking with Grief

Written by Andy Raine and used with permission.
For more information please visit
www.northumbriacommunity.org

Do not hurry
As you walk with grief,
it does not help the journey.
Walk slowly, processing often:
do not hurry
as you walk with grief.

Be not disturbed
by memories that come unbidden
Swiftly forgive, and let Christ speak for you
unspoken words.
Unfinished conversations
will be resolved in him.
Be not disturbed.

Be gentle with the one who walks with grief,
if it is you
be gentle with yourself.
Swiftly forgive;
walk slowly,
pausing often.

GRIEF AND GRACE

Take time, be gentle
as you walk with grief.
Most other griefs are external.
This is internal.
A part of me has died.
The person I was, has died.
The person I was becoming is no more.
Another one lives.

REFLECTION: CHAPTER FIVE

Tim describes three rules he set himself to help him through this phase of the journey. Are there similar rules that have helped you through experiences of grief in the past? Can you think of any rules that may help you in similar experiences in the future?

Tim shares a poem at the end of this chapter. What is your reaction to this poem? What feelings, thoughts or ideas do they stir up? Can you write/draw/create/do something by way of response?

CHAPTER SIX
THE NEW ABNORMAL

23 October 2016

From Bruce Murray quoting Dietrich Bonhoeffer:

There is nothing that can replace the absence of someone dear to us, and one should not even attempt to do so. One must simply hold out and endure it. At first that sounds very hard, but at the same time it is also a great comfort. For to the extent the emptiness remains unfulfilled one remains connected to the other through it. It is wrong to say that God fills the emptiness. God in no way fills it but much more leaves it precisely unfilled and this helps us preserve – even in pain – the authentic relationship. Furthermore, the more beautiful and full the remembrances, the more difficult the separation. But gratitude transforms the torment of memory into silent joy. One bears what was lovely in the past not as a thorn but as a precious gift within, a hidden treasure of which one can always be certain.

Around the time of the memorial service, a number of people used a phrase that I'm not sure I'd come across previously. Many people said that I'd need to find a *new normal*. I knew what they meant. Normal life, as we had known it, had evaporated. Everything had shifted. Our entire world had been turned upside down. Permanently. Things that we'd taken for granted, and the future we were anticipating, had now vanished from sight. There was a discontinuity we were about to face as we stumbled into the future we didn't choose. And in facing that future there was something to be discovered. A new way of doing life that was not disconnected from our past but would still be very different. A *new normal*.

I imagine that the process of discovering a new normal is a common experience for anyone who is going through unanticipated and uninvited loss. The seismic shifts of devastating change may shake the foundation of everything you consider normal. This can cause ripple effects of uncertainty which impacts every area of your life. When a foundational 'normal' is crushed, then there is a very real danger that everything else may crumble and corrode around it. This is what I wrote a few weeks into my new normal:

> 24 September 2016
>
> *As the days go by, I'm increasingly aware that the hole in my life is becoming normal. I don't want it to feel normal that Laura is not here. I don't want to get used to it. I take comfort in that I wake up and reach for her, wishing she was next to me – lie as I once would have done to feel her skin and listen to her breathing in the night. But it's inevitable (I guess) that her missing from our bed will feel the norm*

> *for it is part of my new normal – the normal that I don't want.*
>
> *That was a hard thing about going into work on Thursday. It felt abnormally normal. There was joy in the place and it was good to see everyone. I take great pleasure in what God has done through us at The Message. It felt like it always has. Laura and I loved being part of The Message and I loved going to work… and I was happy being there on Thursday. But part of the [old] 'normal' of work was coming home to Laura – talking to her and being in this together. That's why we loved Eden Salt River so much – it was something we'd birthed together and a foretaste of the future we were anticipating. Our normal life was to be centred on missions, on Africa, on the poor and marginalised. And my pleasure in thinking on that future was that we were going to be together in those things. My normal life revolved around my shared experiences with Laura – and in those shared experiences I found joy and meaning… in the good and bad times.*
>
> *And I want to resist a new normal that doesn't have that. I want to fight against it – and yet I know I'm moving inexorably towards it – because that's the nature of time.*

As I began to take steps into the future we didn't choose, there was an overriding sense that nothing was normal anymore. My sense of *normal* had been laid to rest so building a *new normal* without Laura didn't make sense to me. So, I changed the phrase slightly. I would work towards a *new abnormal.* The new abnormal wasn't just about me. It was primarily about the children and our life as a family. Caleb had said at the memorial service that four seemed like an unwholesome number. In his normal, a family consisted of five people. For the Tucker family, four was unwholesome – it was abnormal. Yet, as we began to live as a family of four, we found a new language to describe our abnormal existence.

I began to speak of us as 'Team Tucker', fostering in us a sense of family unity. We would do activities as Team Tucker, send out prayer requests from Team Tucker, and post the occasional photo on Facebook as Team Tucker. Seeing pictures of just the four of us was an abnormal experience, but an important step in the process of discovering our *new abnormal*.

NAME CHANGE

On one occasion we were sitting at the dinner table discussing the changes that had happened in our lives. We weren't falling into melancholic reminiscences. Rather, Team Tucker were processing our new abnormal. The children had all expressed that they felt their relationship with me was changing. I was now more involved in their lives and, obviously, I'd been taking up some of the tasks that their Mommy had previously done. Although I enjoy cooking, I had previously not cooked every day. Then there was handling the schooling, to which I'd been only a peripheral figure. Another daunting task had been managing the children's social diaries and play-dates. This involved interacting with many Mommys who had complicated algorithms to align their children's schedules (thankfully, I received some good coaching by some super-competent Moms). I thought that I had a handle of complex multitasking in my role as a CEO. But it went to another level as I morphed into a new parenting role.

At the table we were laughing about this. I said that the kids needed to come up with a new name for me because there were times I was being more 'Mom' than 'Dad'. (I apologise to my friends who will struggle with these gender stereotypes... but hey, we were in a new abnormal!) And there were other times when I was still more Dad than Mom. So, we agreed, when I'm more Mom than Dad – then they'd call me MAD. And when I'm more Dad than Mom... then they'd call me DAM. We then realised how appropriate it was that we had appropriately described my disposition in our new abnormal... I am simply *Dam Mad.*

BEING DAM MAD

Being Dam Mad took me into many areas that were outside of my comfort zone.

One of the more challenging aspects of this new role was learning how to manage Erin's hair. As a white male whose idea of a haircut is 'short-back and sides and gel on top'... this was not only a role change, but a cultural education.

We adopted our beautiful daughter when she was two months old. In 2008 it seemed the time was right, and Laura unhesitatingly threw herself into the process. We were now settled in Pretoria and Laura's brother and his wife (who likewise lived in Pretoria at the time) were also entering into the adoption process. It was a special blessing to go through it together with them. They received their daughter, Joy, just a short while before Erin was placed with us. The two cousins have been best friends ever since. We were so thrilled to have a daughter and Laura bloomed as mother of our third child.

There were many aspects to motherhood that Laura flourished in, and now, with a beautiful daughter, Laura wanted to be able to tend to Erin's hair. Now, this may sound quite straightforward. Yet in a cross-cultural adoption, there was a lot about caring for afro-hair that she had no clue about. It was a whole new world which Laura thoroughly embraced. Over the years, she taught herself how to care for Erin's hair. Erin has gorgeous, but extremely tight curls, so washing, combing out and braiding was often a long and painful process which resulted in both daughter and mother ending up in tears. In time, Erin and Laura decided to begin styling her hair into dreadlocks. This would be a lengthy process and so they started going to a salon once a month. These regular trips were a bonding time for them as Laura would sit with Erin through the painful ordeal; fuelling her resilience with snacks and distracting her with movies or games.

In the weeks following Laura's death, I tried to initially ignore the fact that Erin's hair was beginning to look a bit bedraggled. However, it was inevitable that her hair would need tending to and I was determined to follow my *What Would Laura Do* mantra. So, armed with my laptop, movies, sweets and some books, Erin and I went to the salon. She was resistant but knew it was necessary and was determined to be brave. The three-hour session was tough. Erin coped heroically, and I sat by her side trying to adapt to a world that was foreign to me. But I knew I needed to be there for her and it wasn't a task I was ready to delegate to someone else.

Once completed, we paid and walked out of the shop. Then standing there on Main Road in Observatory, Erin dissolved into tears and collapsed into my arms. We were both overwhelmed with the reality of our loss and that this was our new reality. We went to the Spur for some food and daddy-daughter time. It had been tough, but we also knew that Mommy would be proud that we'd faced the challenge and survived.

BALLET DAD

An annual unmissable event was Erin's ballet concert. 12 weeks into our new abnormal, we had to face the first of Erin's performances without Laura being present:

> 10 November 2016
>
> *Yesterday was Erin's ballet concert. A date that Laura had me put in the diary early this year – the date when Daddy has to be present. A date I wouldn't miss for the world. I love watching Erin dance. I wonder if Laura dances with her. I love hearing Erin sing. I wonder if Laura sings with her. I can't be certain, but I hope so (Even if she starts in a too low key like she used to).*
>
> *It was good to be there – I even tried to get closer to the front... that was important to Laura... not just so we'd have a good view – but so that Erin could see us. Danielle came with me which I really appreciated. Erin was so brave. She told me today she was missing Mommy a lot – I'm sure it was connected to the concert – even if she can't articulate it. She's also sleeping in my bed... I guess another sign of her needs at the moment.*

> *I coped OK – although conscious of missing Laura. Even more so because Caleb was sick... again, not my forte – but I'm trying...*

In many respects, the tragedy of our loss came specifically into focus when considering Erin. She had just turned eight when her Mommy died. Laura and Erin had a special bond and I felt ill-equipped to compensate for that loss. How could I? But since the day Erin joined our family and slept on my chest that first night she was home, she has been my princess and delight. She also has Laura's gift of empathy. Throughout my time of deep grief, she took it on herself to often ask how I was doing. We shared in deep pain. We wept together, and we comforted each other. And I determined, by God's grace, to keep the memories that she had of Laura alive. I realised that, as she gets older, these threads of connection to her Mommy will be vital for her sense of rootedness. Therefore, one early decision I made was to buy a journal for each of the children. This could be a space where they could record special memories, Bible verses and write letters to their Mommy. Additionally, I write in the journal on special occasions or when there is a recollection or memory that I feel may be important to the children in the future. The boys have not used the journals very regularly and I trust what I've written there will become helpful to them as they grow older. However, Erin has drawn pictures, written in it, and regularly reads the contents. We also often find her looking at photos or collecting things that have special memories. Each of the children is processing their grief uniquely as they face their new abnormal and this will, no doubt, impact them differently over time. But, as Team Tucker, we do have a common loss that helped us build a shared resilience and strong faith that God is with us even in the most difficult of circumstances. I hope and pray this will enable the children to survive and thrive as they live out their new abnormal.

GRACE

The children were God's means of grace to me on many levels. At Laura's bedside in intensive care, I asked God how they will possibly get through the pain of losing their Mommy. But right there, in that moment of crisis, God spoke to me through one of the nurses. She told me that she had recently married a man who had lost his wife a few years previously. He also had children. She shared that his kids were so well-adjusted and had a depth of maturity she hadn't seen in other children. Although it was very fresh as I wasn't even able to contemplate life without Laura at that point, it was a testimony of grace that I have often reflected on. They were encouraging words from a stranger who I will probably never meet again.

This did become my experience in the months that followed. The crisis we shared began to shape the nature of my relationship with the children. I don't think I was a bad dad previously, but Laura had carried the brunt of day-to-day parental responsibility. In fact, this was a means of grace we could draw on. Just two weeks into our new abnormal, I wrote the following after a visit from close friends who have known the children since birth.

> *1 September 2016*
>
> *An amazing thought from chatting with Colleen and Sam this evening is realising that the kids had more quality time with Laura than many kids have with their mum in a lifetime. So it's no wonder that her grace and love is so etched into their being – something I need to remind them of constantly.*

Initially, having the children close to me was extremely important and part of my coping mechanism. They were God's gift of grace to me and a necessary part of my survival mechanism. I was on tenterhooks when they were not around. I wrote:

> *28 August 2016*
>
> *And the reality of facing the future as a single parent just seems a nightmare that I never anticipated. But all I want is to keep the kids close... as my connection to Laura and also as those I love in some measure [comparably] towards how I love her. Also, to know we're all safe and in this together.*

I was very open with the kids as to what I was going through. I've heard that, in the old days, children were not exposed to the grief of their parents. They didn't attend funerals and were insulated from grief. That certainly wasn't my approach. Team Tucker were in this together. I tried not to dump emotional baggage on them. But they did see me cry, knew my struggles and were exposed to my pain. But I also shared with them the small victories. This might be in the form of a Bible passage, encouraging thought or a moment that brought joy. It was not all doom and gloom in the Tucker house!

One moment that stands out was in the car as we were driving somewhere (I can't remember where). I played a song to the children that had significantly impacted me. This song became a means of grace to us; speaking hope into our lives and helping bring a heavenly perspective to our situation. My journal entry from that day, just over a month after Laura's passing, starts with a Bible verse that had spoken to me (from my daily readings through the Psalms), and then records the lyrics of the song – a song we've listened to many times over the past couple of years:

> *19 September 2016*
>
> *'Stay with God! Take heart. Don't quit. I'll say it again: Stay with God.' Psalm 27:14, MSG*
>
> *I was listening to Passion album – Take it All... one I bought for Laura a couple of years ago. Was blown away by 'Come as you are' by Crowder. These lyrics are so powerful for me at the moment:*
>
> *Come out of sadness from wherever you've been,*
> *Come broken-hearted, let rescue begin,*
> *Come find your mercy, oh sinner come kneel,*
> *Earth has no sorrow that heaven can't heal.*
>
> *So lay down your burdens, lay down your shame,*
> *All who are broken, lift up your face,*
> *Oh wanderer come home, you're not too far,*

> *So lay down your hurt, lay down your heart, come as you are.*
>
> *There's hope for the hopeless and all those who've strayed,*
> *Come sit at the table, come taste the grace,*
> *There's rest for the weary, rest that endures,*
> *Earth has no sorrow that heaven can't cure.*
>
> *There's joy for the morning, oh sinner be still,*
> *Earth has no sorrow that heaven can't heal,*
> *Earth has no sorrow that heaven can't heal.*

There were also times when the children said things that made a profound impact upon me. One occasion in particular stands out.

A friend had loaned us the film *God's Not Dead*. I watched it one evening with the boys. The story is of a Christian student called Shane Harper at college in the USA. His philosophy professor is a devout atheist who pressurises his students to disavow their faith and make the statement that God is dead. Shane refuses to do so and is thus set an assignment by the professor to prove that God does exist.

Shane sets to work on his project but faces mounting opposition from the professor. After one presentation, at which the professor had sarcastically and vindictively undermined him, Shane looks at his professor and asks, '*what happened to you?*' With resentment in his voice, the professor tells of how, as a 12-year-old boy, his mom had been seriously ill. Despite his prayers, his mother had still passed away. God had not intervened. His prayers were unanswered. Therefore, he rejected God and faith. And, by implication, he set his life-mission to undermine and ridicule anyone who deigned to believe in God's existence.

Yes – this was a little bit close to home and an emotional part of the film for us to watch. It's a fictitious story, but perhaps that is many people's experience. Pain and disappointment in life causes them to reject God rather than turn to him and accept his loving embrace. At Laura's bedside, that was my biggest fear when considering the new abnormal that the children would be facing. But it wasn't a fear based in reality.

Caleb, Samuel and Erin have not become bitter or questioned Laura's passing in a negative manner. Rather, they have turned to God and are trusting him. At the end of the movie I told them how proud I am of them and how they had responded to losing their Mommy. I referred to the professor's disillusionment and resentment and how they hadn't chosen to be bitter but continue to trust God. Caleb looked at me and simply said, 'but that guy didn't have a Dad'.

It was a mind-blowing realisation for me. I'd been focused on how the children were a gift of grace to me. Caleb's comment reframed my thinking in that we were a gift of grace to one another. I recognised that they were a lifeline for me and I was their Dad – which is exactly what they needed me to be. As their Dad, I had to lead the way in facing our new abnormal, painful as it was. God had called us to walk this pathway together and we would find a way of facing the future we didn't choose.

This journal entry sums up the mutuality of our relationship. I was Dam Mad. They were our children and Laura's legacy. Grief and Grace all wound up together in our new abnormal.

23 September 2016

Thankful for the relationship with the kids. They are their mother's children and I'm benefiting from her investment in their lives. Laura would be so proud of them – as am I. They are my number 1 priority in this and I think the boys are really benefiting from just the amount of time I've been spending with them. Caleb just said to me that he never really felt the need to get to know me before because he always had Mom with them... but now he's really glad to be with me. Humbling words.

REFLECTION: CHAPTER SIX

Tim describes the 'new normal' as the 'new abnormal'. This is globally now a very familiar term in the wake of the Covid pandemic.

Can you identify any 'new abnormals' that you have adapted to in the wake of grief and loss in your life?

What signs of grace can you point to in those situations, alongside the griefs?

Tim talks about a song that became significant for him. Is there something similar that has helped you in times of enforced change? What specifically about this has been helpful?

CHAPTER SEVEN

RUN WITH A HEAVY HEART

> ...but I know of something that suggests even greater strength; the power to continue working after a setback, the power to still run with a heavy heart, the power to perform your daily tasks with deep sorrow in your spirit. This is a Christlike thing!
>
> GEORGE MATHESON

PUBLIC GRIEF

I am, by nature and nurture, a private person. At least, I thought I was. Certainly, when I was younger, I avoided public demonstrations of emotion. Particularly sad emotions. My grandmother passed away when I was 17. She had cancer and fought bravely. I saw her at the hospital a couple of nights before she died. I read some scripture to her knowing that her time on Earth was drawing to a close. I went from the hospital to a friend's house where we regularly gathered for prayer. I shared a little about my gran and then we spent some time in prayer. During the prayer I broke down in tears. My teenage angst kicked in and I felt an acute sense of embarrassment. I made a decision not to allow myself to cry in public again. It took many years before God broke down my emotional tortoise shell. The point is, I'm not someone who wears my heart on my sleeve. However, in those latter days of August 2016, God mercifully allowed me to grieve publicly without feeling ashamed. In fact, I recognised that losing Laura was not a private matter. I was not the only one grieving but was part of a community of people who keenly felt her loss. This wasn't just about me.

It was with this in mind that I prepared my tribute for the memorial service. I had a few things on my heart as I addressed the task of putting into words something that would honour Laura. The first was that I wanted to be authentic. But I didn't want to dwell in self-pity. The pain really did hurt. But I wanted to express that we had hope. The second was that I wanted to express something of Team Tucker. The children needed to have their say and express themselves in some way. And, thirdly, I wanted to acknowledge that we were part of a broader community. I desired to build bridges to people so that they could feel able to share their own loss and so that we could all find some sense of purpose and direction through the valley we were in.

The children had agreed to stand with me as I gave our tribute. Their courage helped put steel in my spine. My face was flushed from the tears that had been falling so I prayed for strength that I would be able to communicate in a way that would help all of us navigate our way through the valley of the shadow of death. The full text of what I shared is in the appendix, but here are my closing words as I sought to run with a heavy heart:

> We will make it through this time because we have one another, we have all the people who have been supporting us... and we have the Lord. And so, we say, even as we grieve deeply for the loss of Laura and we don't have all the answers... it is well with my soul. The Lord gives, the Lord takes away, the name of the LORD be praised!
>
> As a family we want you to know that we are praying for all of you... that good will come out of this tragedy. Our heart is that you will be able to take stock, recognising that life is fragile and none of us knows what tomorrow will bring... so make the most of today. Ensure that you are in a right relationship with God through Jesus Christ. Seek reconciliation with those you have offended or have offended you. Strengthen your marriages. Appreciate your children. Serve the poor and share God's love with others. Our time is short – but... as Laura's life is a witness to... our impact can be huge.
>
> I'll close with one of her favourite verses which she would be praying for all of us today:
>
> Philippians 4:6-7: Do not be anxious about anything, but in every situation, by prayer and petition, with thanksgiving, present your requests to God. And the peace of God, which transcends all understanding, will guard your hearts and your minds in Christ Jesus.

NAVIGATING RELATIONSHIPS

My experience was that dealing with relationships during a time of loss has many complexities. I found myself oscillating between a need for company, while also wanting to withdraw and be alone. The former was sometimes emotionally draining, while the latter was not always good for my soul. Additionally, I became aware that some people were struggling with their own grief and I would have to be prepared to comfort others. In the early stages it wasn't uncommon for people to be in tears when talking to me. Whether my grief was opening up wounds of their own, or they were simply overwhelmed by the sadness of our situation, I learned that people's reactions were unpredictable. This made me a little cautious of who I would spend time with. While not wanting to offend people, I wasn't ready to be their counsellor.

These various tensions of my experience come through in a fairly lengthy journal entry I made exactly one month after Laura's death. I wrote in two parts… an entry in the morning, and then further reflection in the evening. The entry summarises many of the challenges I've already expressed in previous chapters and highlights the yo-yoing emotional challenges that I was facing.

It also contains two quotes from the Scottish hymn-writer, George Matheson (contained in a devotional book by Angus Buchan), which spoke directly into the challenge I was facing relating to the communal nature of grief. I entirely related to his phrase that I must *run with a heavy heart*. Sometimes I felt like retreating into my shell. And there were appropriate times when I had to do this. However, I ultimately knew that I needed to navigate these relational challenges in a way that included my broader community and opened my heart up to the healing power of loving relationships.

18 September 2016

Yesterday – Laura's parents arrived. It's good to have them here.

Also spoke with Gareth Lloyd Jones... was good to connect with him. I have some incredible friendships – so grateful.

Last night I was in bed watching some junk TV (normally I only watch football or something I've recorded – but was in my room and neither available)... and for the first time I was really frustrated about just doing things that are a waste of time. I don't want to pass hours feeding my brain rubbish in an attempt to 'numb the pain'. And although I realise I'm tired and don't have the capacity I normally have, plus just managing myself, the kids, the home etc. takes a lot of energy, last night I wanted something more than just junk TV. So quite late as it was, I picked up Angus Buchan's book and was amazed that the chapter was essentially on handling grief – and a couple of sections really stood out for me particularly the following quote:

George Matheson on patient endurance: (based on Hebrews 12:1–2)

'We think of it as an angel who guards the bed of the disturbed. But that is not the patience with which the Lord

Jesus Christ is telling us to run the race. There is a much harder patience that we need to obtain, and that is having patience on the run… lying down during a time of grief, or being quiet after a financial setback certainly implies great strength but I know of something that suggests even greater strength; the power to continue working after a setback, the power to still run with a heavy heart, the power to perform your daily tasks with deep sorrow in your spirit. This is a Christlike thing.

'Many of us would tearlessly deal with our grief if only we were allowed to do it in private, yet what is so difficult is that most of us are called to exercise patience, not in a bed, but in the open street for all to see. We are called upon to bury our sorrows not in restful inactivity but in active service; in our workplace, while shopping and doing social events… contributing to other people's joy. No other way of bearing sorrow is as difficult as this, for it is truly what is meant by running with patience.'

The weekends are so hard – particularly Sunday. It's meant to be my time with Laura. Chilling out. Being together. My heart is broken. I miss her so much.

Today was a struggle.

After writing what I did this morning and feeling more positive about trying to still 'run with a heavy heart' – today was exceptionally hard. Church is always overwhelming. And when I sit for the sermon I invariably doze off. I did hang around a bit after the service to collect the kids – but it wasn't easy. Worship is emotional – it's not easy to sing – but I can almost imagine Laura singing in heaven... it's the one time and way that I can feel a connection to her – worshipping God.

Having Laura's folks here is great – but an adjustment. Laura always loved being with parents and buzzed around whenever her Mom was here – I'd even feel left out and joke about it. But they shared a close bond. And I love them as a son and am so grateful to them... and they help so practically... but it has affected me having them here – someone else to consider when I'm trying to keep my head above water. And although we always loved having either set of our parents with us – we always had each other to escape to and debrief with.

And I realised again today that it's not just that I miss having Laura to talk to about the decisions I need to make and the challenges I'm facing – but I miss having her to console me in my grief. Whenever I've been through really tough stuff – she's the one I turn to and, with God uniting us – we got through stuff together. I need her now more than ever... but she isn't here.

And today was a painfully slow day – time ticked by so slowly... and I don't think inactivity helps me... I need to be careful of what may make me feel vulnerable and alone. Today I did.

'HOW ARE YOU?'

In the previous journal entry, I allude to how I struggled with going to church on Sunday. The church we attend, Jubilee Community Church, was an incredible support to us. However, it was initially extremely difficult to go through the motions of attending Sunday services. Now I would arrive shortly after the service had begun and leave as soon as it was completed. I wanted to be amongst people that loved me. But I wasn't ready to engage in conversation. There was always the chance that someone would ask that most dreadful of questions for someone going through deep loss, 'How are you?'. These three words would cause my stomach to churn. Do they really want to know? Should I lie? So, I found it easier to try and avoid it. In my journal I reflect on these challenges.

> *27 September 2016*
>
> *'How are you?'*
>
> *I must admit I typically deflect this question – except to a few trusted friends. I actually don't know how I am. I am grieving. And that's exhausting.*
>
> *I am surviving. Mercifully – somehow, I survive each day.*
>
> *I am missing Laura. There's a hole in my experiences.*
>
> *I am lonely – but I try to keep busy.*

> *I guess people don't really want to hear all of that – or maybe they do because they may want to know I'm human and it isn't getting any easier with time.*

If it was tough engaging with people I did know, it was even harder to meet new people. I tried to avoid conversations with people who didn't know me, Laura or what had happened. I made the following note when we went on our short holiday.

> **9 October 2016**
>
> *But although there are other people, I have no desire to talk to them – in case they ask and I have to explain about Laura. I don't want to talk to people who didn't know her and don't understand the depth of my loss.*

A few weeks later, it was equally difficult. I made this note after I'd been at Erin's ballet concert (as described in the previous chapter):

> **10 November 2016**
>
> *The hardest part was the end... meeting a new couple who seemed really sweet... but who don't know Laura or our situation... something I'm still finding tough – maybe will for a while.*

And yet there was a paradox that I experienced. I needed to talk about Laura with people who knew her well. I didn't desire to become a hermit who disengaged from interacting with other people. Rather, I had a need to connect with people who could, in some way, relate to my loss because of the shared connection we had with Laura.

> *6 November 2016*
>
> *One of the things I've realised is tough is not having people around who openly talk about Laura – who don't have that shared history or long memories. Without family around, I feel unable to connect with people on this. Most of our friends are recent friends – at least the people I see regularly – and they seem reluctant to even mention Laura. It was good to have the Frasers here in the week and actually talk to Danielle about Laura and realise that she is missing her. The kids bring up memories and chat occasionally – but not to any depth. I guess this is one of the challenges of being in Cape Town. It was good to get that one letter from Louise – to the kids – as someone who has an even longer history than I do with Laura. And there's Andrew and Gill. But I think this is something I may have to actively seek out... to have conversations with people about Laura and specific memories of our time together.*

A SHRINKING WORLD

It was tough enough running with a heavy heart in terms of the ongoing relationships with people I saw on a regular basis. But, in the 21st century, there's a whole new dimension to navigating relationships while enduring through grief: the social media revolution.

In 2011, I got a new sense of the impact that social media is having on the world. No longer was Facebook, Twitter etc. a medium through which people simply shared trivial news, goofy photos and birthday wishes to an ever-increasing network of global acquaintances. Rather, I was stunned by how social media had become a globalised space for the sharing of communal grief.

My good friend and colleague, Mark Versey, passed away on 25 February 2011. I vividly remember the moment I heard the news from my dad. I was driving to a church leaders' retreat. The phone rang, and I saw an international number on the screen. It was my dad calling from the UK. I pulled over to the side of the road. He shared with me the tragic news that Mark had passed away. He was just 38 years old. His death was a sudden and uninvited interruption into mine and hundreds of other people's lives. Mark was a very special person.

I had known Mark for seven years. He was a single guy who had a passion for God, for people, for travel and for football. All of these passions combined in his perfect job when he joined Ambassadors in Sport (AIS). At the time, I was leading the South African branch of AIS with the responsibility to develop the work into other African countries. Mark was based out of the UK and part of his job was to recruit and mobilise people to serve on our international football tours. Our worlds first collided when we worked together to organise and lead a football tour to Zambia in 2005. Mark was full of faith for the tour and recruited a great team of people. A residing memory of the tour was when we played a match in Livingstone. The locals came to watch and were at first amused by Mark's slightly portly physique. But he was a canny and surprisingly pacey defender who won tackle after tackle against the nimble Zambian team. Mark won the crowd over and they were soon cheering his every move. That was Mark. 100% committed to everything he did. Passionate, affable, good-humoured and gifted.

Over the next few years we also worked on projects in Senegal and Ghana together. Mark was a networker par-excellence, but with a unique gift. He didn't just connect the right people to the right opportunities. He also built lasting friendships and remained in touch with people beyond their two- or three-week experience with AIS, even recruiting a number of people to join the organisation in permanent positions.

When, in 2008, I was looking for someone to project manage our 2010 FIFA World Cup outreach across South Africa, Mark was top of my list. Our UK branch reluctantly agreed to second him to us, and he moved to Pretoria and joined our full-time staff team. Working with Mark was one of the highlights of my years with AIS. During 2010, Mark and I facilitated football events across the country and people arrived from around the world to serve alongside us, creating unforgettable experiences for dozens of people. After the World Cup, Mark returned to the UK and was appointed leader of our London office. He would only serve in that position for a few months.

As I began to digest the news of Mark's death, I was aware that it would cause ripple effects around the world. In a bit of a daze, I managed to continue our drive to the retreat centre where we were having our meetings. I was thinking of all the people I'd need to contact and was dreading sharing the news. When we got to the centre I managed to get online and also started making calls.

As I browsed my Facebook, I began to see my news feed filling up with messages that tagged Mark. Tribute after tribute was being posted. Photos of Mark with friends from many countries around the world. Some were expressing their raw grief – having heard the news from someone else's post. Others had received a phone call and were going online in disbelief, seeking to connect with others who were also grappling with the tragic news. I felt a bit stunned as I witnessed this global expression of grief. It was an amazing testimony to the impact that Mark's life had had. And it was also an incredible comfort to be able to relate to a global community of people through the shrinking world brought about by social media.

The breaking of tragic news via social media seems to now be part of everyday life. In 2011 it was the first time I became aware of how this could be a powerful medium to help people through their grief. However, an equal and opposite danger has emerged: that tragedy is becoming commonplace and we therefore become desensitised to our newsfeeds. In the same browsing session, we can see acquaintances or far-flung friends celebrating an engagement or the birth of a baby, while others are announcing that they have cancer or have lost a job. This phenomenon of desensitisation used to merely apply to global tragedies that we read about in the newspaper or watched unfold on TV News. But now, at any point of any day, our lives can be interrupted with uninvited heart-breaking news as friends and loved ones, or even long-lost acquaintances, experience and share their personal trials and grief.

The reality is that social media is here to stay, and it is a vehicle of communication that I needed to navigate as I managed my own grief. Some people lay their hearts bare for all to read through highly personal and emotive posts. I knew that wouldn't be my style and I determined to try and use the platform sensitively and sparingly. It was certainly a comfort to read other people's tributes to Laura and messages of love that came through various online platforms. Some friends collated the tributes and included them in one of the books of remembrance that we were given in the weeks after Laura's death. So, although I browsed regularly, I posted sparingly. The posts I did place on social media were either of Team Tucker hiking, surfing and showing us adjusting to our new abnormal life. I also posted on special memorial days, such as Laura's birthday. At these times I knew there would be other people thinking of Laura, praying for us, and processing their own grief. It was special to be able to reach out and share in those moments with others who somewhat understood what we were going through.

One positive and helpful thing I did was to form two WhatsApp groups. One was for family. And the other of trusted friends. To the latter I posted regular requests for prayer for personal matters that I would not have wanted to share more broadly. The group was a gift of grace as it enabled me to connect with good friends at times when I felt most vulnerable or was facing my biggest challenges.

Perhaps the jury is still out on whether social media is a force for good or evil, whether it helps or hinders during deep loss. However, as I sought to run with a heavy heart it was a community that did ultimately play a positive role in helping me process my grief.

GRACE: GIFTS ALONG THE WAY

How to engage with family, friends and the broader community is a challenge of running with a heavy heart that will look differently for each person facing loss. As a Christian, I took tremendous comfort from the knowledge that hundreds of people were not just feeling some measure of the pain we felt but were turning that pain into prayers for us. I heard of one family in the UK who fasted and prayed for us every Thursday for a full year. Remarkable!

Ultimately, as a Christian, my faith and hope is in my relationship with God, a topic I will explore further in the coming chapters. However, I came to see the community of people around me as gifts that God had given me to help me through my journey of pain. Just as I don't see my relationship with God as a crutch, but a gift of grace, so God used people as *gifts along the way*.

My community of friends in Cape Town helped us practically. For weeks after Laura's death, we had people arrive at our house with meals. Danielle had used an app to coordinate who would bring what meal on which day. The kids joked that it's a good job they like lasagne, as we sometimes had it for several days in a row. But it was a practical way that people helped us. It was a gift along the way. It wouldn't be healthy if I was still receiving meals every day – if I'd become dependent on these acts of kindness. The time came when I said to Danielle that I was ready to handle the task of cooking for us. Gifts along the way move people from crisis, into survival, and then into their new abnormal.

It was the same with another gift along the way. A couple of weeks after Laura's passing, I met with a counsellor at our church. I'd never had formal counselling before, but my conversations with Kyle were extremely helpful and gave me certain perspectives I wouldn't have otherwise obtained. And, likewise, with medical help. Initially I avoided sleeping tablets, but a doctor friend had given me some 'just in case'. At one point I got so exhausted from lack of sleep that I decided to take a tablet. I remember the feeling I had when I woke up the next morning from a good night's sleep – utter relief! Medical assistance is clearly a gift of grace that people facing trauma, crisis and grief should seek out. As a Christian I believe that God has enabled medical professionals to be a gift of grace that provide essential help to those of us in need.

So, I learned a beautiful thing. Although it was tough to run with a heavy heart, people became the source of God's gracious gifts that helped me along the way. And this led to some breakthroughs at various stages; glimpses of light breaking through my smog.

14 November 2016

Today worked through two more challenges. Firstly, shared publicly for the first time at Prayer Day. Was good to address the team and also to share what God has been doing. Closed with 1 Cor. 15:56-57... key verses as we look ahead to God's calling next year and beyond.

The second thing was chatting to strangers... both at prayer day where I managed to, briefly, share the Gospel with Michael. And then at Pinelands High School... was chatting to another Dad and got to mention about Laura dying. Will that become easier? Not sure. But managed to say the words – and that seemed like a breakthrough.

REFLECTION: CHAPTER SEVEN

Tim talks about 'running with a heavy heart' and how this specifically impacted upon his relationship with other people. How do you identify with this experience?

Is there another way you might express it?

How do you respond when people ask, 'How are you?'

CHAPTER EIGHT

TWO SIDES OF THE SAME COIN

> O joy that seekest me through pain, I cannot close my heart to thee;
> I trace the rainbow through the rain, And feel the promise is not in vain,
> That morn shall tearless be.
>
> GEORGE MATHESON

YES, LORD?

Nigeria is a country that does things on a scale that I've never experienced anywhere else. In 2003 I was invited to go to Lagos and attend the Holy Ghost Convention by the Redeemed Christian Church of God (RCCG). It was an unforgettable trip for many reasons, but one memory is etched on my mind. Every evening there was a gathering in the main auditorium at the heart of 'Redemption

Camp', the mini-city that hosts the RCCG mega-gatherings. Approximately 750,000 people were at this gathering. It's hard to describe the structure where they meet. The auditorium is a kilometer-long open warehouse, packed with white chairs as far as the eye can see. The venue buzzed with anticipation. As a visiting guest (ostensibly there to give sports ministry training at other times during the conference) I was always allocated a chair on the front row. The evening began with praise and worship. I didn't know many of the songs that were sung by the choir and reverberated through the edifice, but there was one that was familiar to me. *I'm trading my sorrows...* the song began... *I'm trading my shame, I'm laying them down for the joy of the Lord*. Then, as we reached the chorus, which simply repeats the refrain *Yes Lord, Yes Lord, yes, yes Lord,* the decibels rose as faith was being stirred amongst the congregation. I turned to look around and, as far as the eyes could see, the white plastic chairs were being held aloft of people's heads and being pumped into the air. Joy, faith, and hope were bursting into the atmosphere... a scene incomparable to anything I've witnessed at any rock concert or global sporting event.

This song, written by Darrell Evans, is a Christian anthem of hope based on Psalm 30:5b which says, 'weeping may stay for the night, but rejoicing [joy] comes in the morning'. The psalm writer goes on to declare to God, 'You turned my wailing [mourning] into dancing; you removed my sackcloth and clothed me with joy.' The implication of the song is that there is a trade-off. We lay down suffering, pain, illness in the anticipation that we will receive joy. The resounding chorus of '*yes Lord*', is a hearty *Amen* to this process.

I'm not opposed to singing the song as it is a stirring rallying call to faith in God in all of life's circumstances. However, the danger of interpreting the psalm in terms of a trade-off is that it implies that sorrow and happiness, mourning and dancing, pain and joy, are linear experiences in life. The implication is that, as we go through life, there will be times of hardship and suffering, but then we simply trade those for times of blessing. It further suggests that we should be seeking to escape pain and grief. Do we only say 'yes' to God when he gives us blessing? Or is there a place for saying 'yes' to him during times of pain – when everything inside us wants to scream at him 'No Lord, No Lord, no, no no!' After all, isn't that what Jesus did in the Garden of Gethsemane? When contemplating the cross everything within him wanted to make a trade. But, in spite of wanting to say 'no', he still said 'yes – not my will, but yours be done' (see Luke 22:39-42).

My experience is that pain and joy are not two separate phases of life that we traverse between. Rather, they are often intertwined in our daily experience. They are two sides of the same coin. Pain in the night, joy in the morning. Grief and dancing are not mutually exclusive. Certainly, when Laura died, everything in me wanted to scream 'no Lord', this is too much to bear. But I had to learn to say 'yes' to the journey, and, in so doing, I learned more about the coexistence of joy and pain. Perhaps the best way I can explain this is my personal translation of Psalm 30:11: 'you turned my mourning in to *surfing*.'

TURNING MOURNING IN TO SURFING

As I have mentioned previously, soon after Laura's death I bought a journal for each of the children. As opportunity arose, I asked each close family member to write something in each of their journals respectively. My dad spent some time in thought and prayer before writing his personal message to the children, including a memory of their mom and also a photo that captured a specific moment.

One of the photos he chose was of when they had come with us to the beach during their last visit to us while Laura was still alive. It was Easter, 2016. Over the past year we had booked surfing lessons for the kids and they had all learned the basics of how to catch a wave and stand on their board. So, on this occasion, we went to surfers' corner in Muizenberg, hired a couple of surf boards and the children demonstrated their new-found talent to their admiring grandparents. All of us were in the shallows of the water, cheering them on. But, the most enthusiastic of us, was Laura. She celebrated every triumphant surf with arms aloft, cheering the children along. My dad caught one such moment on camera. Laura, in her element, in the shallows of the surf. Broad smile on her face and delight in her eyes, as one of the children came cruising in on a wave towards her.

The picture captures the definition of joy. The journey home from Muizenberg to Observatory was one of contentment and laughter as we recalled the successes and humorous highlights of the day.

Just six months later I was driving back from Muizenberg to Observatory again. We were now a family of four, an unwholesome number as per Caleb's observation. We'd had a session of daddy-home-schooling. We'd been at the beach.

The kids had been surfing. It was the second time we'd been surfing. On the first occasion I simply recalled the following in my journal:

> **16 September 2016**
>
> *Turning mourning into dancing – well, not really… but surfing maybe!*
>
> *It's 4 weeks ago today. Rather than mope around our empty house – we went surfing. As Ruth said – Laura would approve. And it was great being in the water – watching them catch waves. Then a seal came and swam a few metres from Sammy and I – God's 'seal of approval!'*
>
> *So maybe we won't turn mourning into dancing – but we'll turn it into surfing –and other things (like giving) that will help us get through this – as a friend of Jesus, not in enmity to him.*

But after the second surfing session I wrote of the void of sadness that had followed that session:

> **21 September 2016**
>
> *This morning we had 'beach school' again. The time in the water, watching the kids, is possibly my favourite time of the week. I'm so engrossed and taking pleasure in them that the cloud lifts. Laura comes/drifts into my mind occasionally – but in the form of a knowledge that she would approve and be loving it.*

But then there's the car journey home. I didn't realise it last week – but looking back the void was there. Today I felt it... all I wanted was her next to me – to relive the surfing with her and debrief in pleasure. To talk of our love for the beach and how well the kids are doing with their surfing...

So it was a mixed bag today. Great to surf with the kids and happy to make some progress with schooling options (and see God answer prayers that we have options) – but aware of the void that has been left.

I'd spent ages with them in the water, cheering them on, trying to help with my limited knowledge of surfing. They'd been catching waves. I knew Laura would be proud and I sensed her approval. There were smiles on the children's faces. I tasted joy. But it didn't last. The drive home was painful. In fact, the pain was accentuated because of the glimpse of joy. My sense of loss was magnified because I didn't have Laura to share the moment with me.

This was a journey of discovery for me. The inter-relationship between pain and joy. It meant I had to make a choice. Do I dare to do things that may bring moments of joy only to have them dissipate due to the realisation of heightened grief? Or do I learn to live with dulled senses – avoid extremes and focus on self-preservation?

Henri Nouwen wrote:

> 'If I am able to remember loneliness during joy, I might be able in the future to remember joy during loneliness and to be stronger to face it and help others face it.'

As I faced the future I didn't choose, I knew that I didn't want to live a joy-less life. Laura wouldn't want me to live a joy-less life. I chose to try and 'remember joy' during loneliness, even though it would also amplify the pain.

As a consequence, the decision to turn mourning into surfing extended beyond merely taking the children surfing. I decided it was high time that I learned to surf! So, in January 2017, I took a borrowed board and wetsuit, and made Muizenberg my surrogate home. The children were now in school, so I had time on my side (and didn't have to embarrass myself in front of them in the water). I learned to stand up on a surfboard. It enabled me to remember joy. I felt Laura's pleasure and imagined her on the beach cheering me on, smiling with me, laughing at me. I sensed her delight that I would choose to do this. I also acutely felt her loss. I mourned. And I surfed.

THE DEMENTORS

Another metaphor I had for the contrast between joy and pain came from the Harry Potter series of books. I wrote:

> *1 October 2016*
>
> *Tough day but got through it...*
>
> *In fact, quite a week all round – with the schooling progress... plus passports arrived. Today was packing for our holiday. So many reminders of Laura. She always packed for the kids – so that was tough enough...*

> *So today has been tough... and now we're packed and just like the adventure to come, I don't get to share the experience with the one person that I really want to. I've realised that these things are like an encounter with the Dementors from Harry Potter – the joy is sucked out of them... the joy I took for granted.*

Some of the fascination with magic and the dark aspects of Harry Potter made me decide that I didn't want the children reading the books or watching the films without my involvement. I read the books over a three-year period to our boys, and then started reading them again to Erin when she was old enough. Despite some of my misgivings, I must admit that we all thoroughly enjoyed the books and it was a great bonding time with the children.

The Dementors are the guards of Azkaban – a special prison for people from the wizarding world. They are amongst the darkest creatures of JK Rowling's imagination. Dementors feed on human happiness, draining the soul of joy. In one scene from the Harry Potter films, the Dementors are attacking Harry and trying to give him the Dementor's Kiss, which would have consumed his soul and left him an empty shell of a person. Horrible! Thankfully, Harry had been taught how to cast a spell that protected him from the Dementors. The Patronus charm is conjured through recalling and focusing on your happiest memory.

I really don't want to take this metaphor too far. However, this is how I felt at times. Whenever we experienced fun or happiness, the sixth sense of grief (as described in chapter 5) kicked in and would try to suck the joy out of the moment. I imagine this is a common experience of those in deep grief or extreme sadness. Joy is sucked out of life leaving one prone to desperation and depression. However, looking back over my period of grief, I did find my own form of a Patronus charm. It wasn't through channelling one particularly happy memory. Rather, it involved stringing together beads of memories formed around gratitude.

GRACE THROUGH GRATITUDE

Rick Warren, author of global best-seller *The Purpose Driven Life*, uses slightly different language to what I've used in this chapter. Whereas I speak of joy and pain as two sides of the same coin, he speaks of battles and blessings as two tracks on the same railway line. Blessings and battles, joy and pain, do not run successively, but rather concurrently as parallel tracks in our journey through life.

Clearly, life after Laura was a battle for me and it was hard to see any flip side of blessing. Pain was the predominant emotion. However, I decided that I would hang on to the hope that joy could be restored. I didn't prescribe what this would look like and I wasn't interested in a 'happy-ever-after' story, but I also wanted to express faith that God could redeem my pain, and that I'd rediscover his purpose for the future I didn't choose. Just eight days after Laura's death I verbalised this in a poem of faith:

> 26 August 2016
>
> *A week is a very long time.*
> *In a moment, everything can change.*
> *Gratitude is the greatest gift.*

> *I can learn to be grateful even in the middle of my loss.*
> *It will take longer for me to recover my joy.*
> *However, because of gratitude, I will still be able to rejoice.*
> *And then maybe healing will come.*
> *And in time... joy.*

I decided I needed to start recording the things I was grateful for and turn them into prayers of thanks. I started with Laura. In my journal I began to list all the things that I had to be thankful for during our 16 years of marriage... including all the little/secret memories that were special only to us. I was partly wanting to ensure that my memories didn't evaporate and that I had a record of the life we shared. But I also needed to remember that, although my situation was devastatingly sad, I still had much to be thankful for. It turns out that gratitude was the greatest gift of grace. Gratitude helped me hold the two-sided coin of joy and pain in tension. Although the coin was mostly pain-side-up at this time, gratitude enabled me to flip it occasionally to experience moments of joy.

In December 2017 I was at a small Methodist church in Milton Keynes. It was a traditional service with songs being sung out of a hymn book. We sang a song that wasn't familiar to me – both in terms of the tune and the old-English language. The hymn was 'O love that wilt not let me go' by George Matheson (I've only recently made the connection between the hymn and the quotes of the previous chapter). George Matheson, a Scottish vicar and hymn-writer, lost his sight as a young man. Upon hearing that Matheson was going completely blind, his fiancée called off their engagement. He never married. On the eve of his sister's wedding, he wrote the hymn. The third verse contains these words:

> O joy that seekest me through pain,
> I cannot close my heart to thee;
> I trace the rainbow through the rain,
> And feel the promise is not in vain,
> That morn shall tearless be.

As I sang these words my heart melted, and tears welled up in my eyes. This described the previous 18 months for me. The two sides of the same coin were ultimately held together because I had faith that God's greater purposes were at work... that he had promised to be with me through thick and thin, in the battle and in the blessing.

The hymn reminded me of Hebrews 12:2 which says of Jesus: 'for the joy set before him, he endured the cross'. I recalled that it is because of my sin that Jesus endured the cross. My pain, and the pain of the whole of humanity was on his shoulders. The Bible says that, at any point, he could have called legions of angels to rescue him. Yet, he endured. He was separated from the godhead and suffered the wrath of God that I deserved. Yet, he endured. He was innocent, and the victim of injustice. Yet, he endured. Why? Because he had traced the rainbow through the rain. He knew the promises of God were not in vain. There was joy set before him... the joy of knowing that what he was going through was going to result in ultimate victory.

I don't think Jesus was happy when he was on the cross. He even cried out 'My God, My God, why have you forsaken me'. But it was the assurance of future joy that kept him nailed to the cross. The promise that his pain would be redeemed – providing *the* answer to all humanity's pain.

As I reflected in gratitude on what Jesus had done, it helped me gain a fresh perspective on my own life and my own story of pain.

And so, it's now important to share more about my faith and my relationship with God during this period.

REFLECTION: CHAPTER EIGHT

Tim describes some complexities in a worship song, the use of verses like Psalm 30:5(b), and how we deal with both blessings and pain. What's your reaction to what Tim talks about here?

Do you think it's possible to say 'Yes' [to God] during times of pain?

The Pixar film *Inside Out* imagines the emotions we experience as characters that live in our heads. The central character is a girl who has moved to a new city with her family; she thought Sadness was something to be avoided, but as the film progresses, she learns that Sadness is an important part of life and can even be a friend.

How do you respond to this idea? Have you ever experienced this to be true?

What comfort, if any, do you take from Hebrews 12:2, and what Tim writes about it?

CHAPTER NINE
MY ALLY, NOT MY ENEMY

> Frodo: I wish the ring had never come to me... I wish none of this had happened.
>
> Gandalf: So do all who get to see such times. But that is not for them to decide. All we have to decide is what to do with the time that is given to us. There are other forces at work in this world besides evil. Bilbo was meant to find the ring, in which case you were also meant to have it... and that is an encouraging thought, is it not.
>
> THE FELLOWSHIP OF THE RING

JEALOUSY

So where was God in all of this? How did my faith shape my response to this tragedy? Or, rather, how did walking through this tragedy shape my faith?

I mentioned in chapter 4 that my prayer at Laura's bedside was simply, '*Lord, everything I've believed since childhood had better be true*'. Maybe it was a child-like or a childish prayer. But right then I needed a father. A daddy. And I called out to my heavenly father desperately hoping that he would give me the faith and resilience to survive the storm.

Laura passed away at 8.30 in the morning and a couple of hours later I was back at the holiday centre where we were staying. The news had been circulated and friends and family were traveling from various places to come and join us. While waiting, I went for a walk around the grounds of the centre – just needing some space and time alone. My mind was a bit numb and the gravity of what had just taken place was slowly beginning to sink in. My emotional turmoil was in stark contrast to the serene surroundings and incredible ocean views. At one point I stood still and tried to reflect on what I was feeling. I thought about God. Was I meant to feel angry with him for taking Laura too soon? Should I be resentful that this had happened to me? But my mind didn't dwell on those things. Rather, I had two primary thoughts.

The first was that I hated death. Death is horrible. I had never felt this hatred for death before. Particularly the death of someone who still had so much to give. She still had so much life to live, and still had so many people to love. I had not invited death to visit my world and turn it upside down. But it came, unprepared as I was. And it occurred to me that death was not God's plan. He hates death. And I wondered how he feels when, on a moment by moment basis, the creatures that he loves so much, have their life on this earth extinguished through a myriad of tragic events. 'Wow', I prayed, 'that must cause you so much pain'. And then it dawned on me that God was not celebrating that Laura had died. He never intended for a man to be left as a widower and for three children to grow up without their mother. No. God understood my pain for this was not his plan for human beings. He also understood my pain because, in order to defeat the consequences of death, he had watched his only Son die on the cross. This is what I'd believed since childhood. The truth of this historical fact had shaped my life. And now, when it mattered most, I didn't feel disconnected from God. Instead, I felt that perhaps I could relate to him a bit better. We shared in this moment of grief. I realised that God was my ally, not my enemy. He was with me in the valley of the shadow of death.

But then I had a second thought which I felt even more keenly. '*God*', I cried, '*I'm jealous*!' You see, I always knew that Laura loved Jesus more than she loved me. But I'd hoped to have her with me for a little while longer – perhaps even into old age.

Laura had become a Christian as a child. Her parents didn't raise her as a Christian, but she did have some exposure to Bible teaching at the local Sunday school. Laura was a sickly child. She nearly lost her life to chronic asthma. Her mom would sit by her bedside in hospital as Laura struggled to breathe. But her tenacious resilience meant she survived. However, from a young age, she had a fear of death. Until, one night, when facing intense fear, she cried out to Jesus. The fear vanished and was replaced by peace and love. Laura trusted in Jesus from that moment on. Her brother, mother and then her father, all, in turn, placed their faith in Jesus and became committed followers of Christ.

Laura had a unique and deep relationship with God. At various points in her life it was expressed through her artistic talent and also through her empathy and concern for others. Unlike many people who become Christians as children, she never had any periods of deep doubt or rebellion. She faithfully served God her whole life. Therefore, it was no surprise that her last words were to cry out to Jesus while we drove to the hospital. He was her closest friend. The lover of her soul.

And I always knew that I just had Laura on loan. I said to the Lord, '*you were always going to have Laura for all eternity, why couldn't you have let me be with her for a little time longer*?' I was jealous. Our marriage had been cut short. But even in that moment there was great comfort. Because God was my ally, I knew how much he loved Laura. We had that in common!

I'M NOT GIVING UP, 'CAUSE YOU'RE NOT GIVING UP

That brief moment and those initial thoughts had a big impact on how I processed my faith and my relationship with God in the coming months. Did I always feel God close to me? No. Was I in constant prayer and communion with him? Of course not. Was reading the Bible, praying, going to church just par for the course? Absolutely not. Everything changed. And do I have all the answers now? No way. But, I did have an assurance that, with God as my ally, I wasn't alone.

I wrote this prayer a few days after Laura's death:

> *23 August 2016*
>
> *Father. I'll never understand why this has happened, but my heart and mind choose to trust you.*
>
> *I trust in you that this is for Laura's best. That she is now with you, in no pain and in complete joy.*
>
> *I trust in you to take care of Caleb, Sammy and Erin for this is a task that's too big for me. I pray that you will shepherd them as a tender-hearted mother.*
>
> *I trust you with my broken heart.*
>
> *We were one. I am no longer whole, but I will find my healing in you.*
>
> *I trust you with my confused mind that you will bring peace to my lack of understanding.*
>
> *I trust you with my future that looks so foggy and uncertain.*
>
> *I trust you to guide me even though I no longer have Laura to consult and walk this journey with me. Amen.*

I was greatly comforted by the thought that I had an ally walking with me through this dark period of my life. Although I had doubts and fears, I couldn't give up on God because I knew he wasn't going to give up on me. A Rivers & Robots song that I listened to a couple of months later accurately expressed my heart:

I commit my way to you, Oh Lord,
For you are the restorer of this world,
My hope is in the name of the Lord Most High.

I delight myself in you, oh Lord,
For you have not forsaken me at all,
My hope is in the name of the Lord Most High.

I'm not giving up, cause you're not giving up.
I'm not giving up, cause you're not giving up.

Though the wicked come and evil may arise,
You surround my heart on every side,
My hope is in the name of the Lord Most High.

I know my inheritance will come,
And righteousness will shine forth like the sun,
My hope is in the name of the Lord Most High.

I put my trust in you, I put my trust in you,
My cloud by day, my fire by night.
I'm not giving up, cause you're not giving up.

THE FAITH JOURNEY THROUGH THE LENS OF MY JOURNAL

In reviewing my journal, there was an intense period of a few weeks when I reflected quite deeply on how my faith intertwined with my grief. Throughout this period, there are references from the Psalms which helped shape a lot of what I was reflecting upon. I had started reading the Psalms immediately after Laura's passing. We were still in George and I was not able to sleep. I woke up and instinctively reached for my Bible. My mind and heart resisted. So, I stood up, turned on the light, and turned to Psalm 1. I read aloud – something I haven't done often in my devotional life. My logic was simple… even if I can't take it in at this time, it simply has to do me good to read God's word. And so, I continued to read through the Psalms… and, as I look back on my journal, there are a number of entries that either simply quote a verse from the psalms, or explore the themes contained more deeply.

The next few paragraphs give a real-time insight into how I was processing my relationship with God at this time. I feel it important to let the entries speak for themselves rather than me give a perspective that may have been modified by time!

> **11 September 2016**
>
> *I'm still reading through the Psalms. Some are comforting and amazing – but some are really tough to read. Like Psalm 41 – David and an appeal to God for healing because of his righteousness – that restoration of health was assured… because of God's mercy, love and because of David's acts of kindness. But the case doesn't fit with regards to Laura. She cared for the weak, sought the Lord, was faithful and righteous, and yet she died. It seems an act of injustice and inconsistent with the revelation of this psalm. The imposter, which is death, does win. Yes, Laura is in heaven and God is in control, but it appears that the enemy does win.*

And yet, it doesn't mean God is not loving, kind or true to his word. David's perspective presents human logic and reason. I'm having to accept that God sovereignly acts beyond my logic, reason, emotions and will. This doesn't seem fair… but my limited understanding and perspective means I don't see the whole picture. Nevertheless, my feelings and hurt are still real and in focus – the loss is deep and the wounds raw. What I really need is God to meet me with his tender love and mercy where I'm at… to feel his presence and be assured by his grace – rather than pontificate on the theology of it all. 'Lord – be in my heart I pray'. And it is the psalms that draw me into his presence and that are most comforting and helpful at this time – those that take me beyond human circumstances.

12 September 2016

Thought for the day: Death is an enemy. God hates death more than I do! He hates it so much that he sent Jesus. When Jesus died God was in agony – mourning deeply! God hates that Laura has died and the pain it causes us. That's why he went through what he went through in order to provide an eternal solution and defeat death.

15 September 2016

I'm not angry with God. In fact, I don't get the whole angry with God thing. I don't understand him – but this whole sin and death thing is not his fault. I'm angry with death. I'm angry that I'm a sinner and couldn't live perfectly with my bride forever – I would've liked that. But how can I be angry with God who keeps loving me, sent Jesus for me and consoles me in my deepest grief because he is constantly grieving with his beloved children who die without knowing him.

No – God is an ally in my grief – and that's the most comforting thing. He gets it. He loved Laura more than me and loves us so much that I'm sure he is weeping over our loss.

17 September 2016

'Father, my ally in grief. My companion [though sometimes unfelt] in pain. My counsellor [through words unspoken] in sackcloth and ashes. My comforter [though not in platitudes and clichés] in the knowledge that you are the suffering God. Please be my healer though not through escape but simply through survival.'

19 September 2016

...my walk with God through this is unique. I don't experience him as the silent observer that C.S. Lewis did. No. Silent, he's not. He is in the pain, sharing in my loss. In empathy. I identify with him in my pain because I've never experienced the pain that he has... and so I draw closer to him in my loss. Not silent. I hear him cry, his screams at death, his anger at sin, his tears mingled with mine...

...what happened is irrevocable and irreversible. The curse of death. Like the smashing of a glass, the denting of the car through a rushed action, the missing of a penalty kick... but oh... a million times worse. The moment happened and cannot be changed.

And yet... and yet... if all I had was that irrevocable and irreversible moment when we switched off her life support machine, then I would be the most desperately depressed man in the world. An object of pity as I'd have lost my lover and best friend for ever. And yet I am not desperate and depressed. I am sad. I am lonely. But because God has cried his own tears of grief – I have hope that ultimately, Jesus has revoked and reversed the curse of death.

And so... in my better moments of this terrifying journey, I have glimpses of hope... that in a blink of an eye in the future everything will change for me and restore me to the joy God intended.

> *In the meantime, I'll continue to survive, to remember and to wish that this had not happened. I will imagine her presence is still with me and consider the future that is now lost to me... while walking into a new future which will have some joy, surprises and delight, as well as more hurt, pain and sorrow... for I am still alive and called to live, not die.*

THE SHACK

I was at a friend's house and, as I often do, I was looking at their bookshelf. I love books but, in the aftermath of my wife's passing, I hadn't had capacity to read that much. I had just about managed to read C.S. Lewis' *A Grief Observed*. But, on this occasion, a book grabbed my attention. I'd heard of *The Shack* by William Young, but it had never really appealed to me. I knew that, in some circles, it was considered theologically weak. However, I read the back cover, and thought 'Hmmm, maybe I should read it'. I then put it back on the shelf.

The next day I was walking through Observatory. On the road between my house and the Spar (where we pick up our emergency groceries... things like snacks, sweets and cooldrink), there is a man with a second-hand bookstall. As I passed, I saw a copy of *The Shack*. 'Interesting', I thought. On my way back from the Spar, I purchased the book. I then devoured it over the next few days. Although I found some of the dialogue frustrating and I didn't necessarily agree with the theological perspective of the author, God did speak to me in a profound way through some of the narrative.

The story is of a man encountering God in the shack where his daughter had been murdered. The chief parallel between my situation and the book was that it was about a man who was grappling with his faith in the light of a devastating tragedy. Although I hadn't anticipated it, God met with me through that book. It was a gift of grace, something that helped me along the way. I noted the following in my journal:

> **26 November 2016**
>
> *Since reading The Shack, I've been thinking – and want to consider further – of how God is meeting with me in this time? Kyle asked me a similar question on Thursday at my counselling session. The main thing I get out of The Shack is how God meets us personally, uniquely and individually – all the time – but particularly during times of grief. It's the Psalm 139 thing – he knows us intimately. The question is – do I perceive him? Am I looking, listening, feeling, smelling and tasting him? Do I allow him to meet with me (in the sense of giving him the time – or just ignoring him)? My ongoing danger is of time-filling and self-sufficiency. However, even in that I can still see God's condescension.*
>
> *Then on Thursday I went for a run and was listening to Muse. I've been storing songs on YouTube that have either spoken to me or were special to Laura and me. As I was listening to Muse I remembered their song 'endlessly' – a song that spoke to me of my commitment to Laura [and made a mental note that I should look it up when I got home and add it to the playlist]. And then, just as I was getting home – the song came on and it was like God was saying 'this is one way I'm*

meeting with you'. It was an emotional moment… a reminder that I need to have ears that hear, eyes that see – to sense how he's meeting me in different ways and through different mediums.

In this time, he's not just met me through [books and] music – but primarily through the children… they've been my saving grace. He's met me through the kindness of others. He's met me through photos and memories of Laura as I've learned to be grateful. He's met me through the home and the things we're doing to honour Laura. He's met me by providing a plan and enabling me to follow through on the plan. He's met me in my studies… they are more than simply a distraction – but something the Holy Spirit has led me in and I need to recognise that. He's met me in provision, through his Word and through the loving support of others.

Of course, the word 'met' is a complete understatement… he's been with me in the sea, on the mountain and when I'm running. Even though I'm slow to acknowledge it – HE IS THERE… and I see it now!

GRACE: AN ETERNAL PERSPECTIVE

I've always believed that having an eternal perspective makes a massive difference to how I live each day. Living in the light of the knowledge that there is a heaven and a hell, inspires me to seek how I can live my life in a way that matters most. As I stated in chapter four, I do not believe that eternal life is 'pie in the sky when I die'. It is not a fairy tale that helps me escape the realities of suffering in the here and now. Rather, my belief in heaven and hell motivates me to be a person who will make a practical difference while still on Earth. My driving passion is to help people discover their purpose by wholeheartedly following Jesus. I believe that people who wholeheartedly follow Jesus change the world on a daily basis.

In addition, my belief in eternal life helped me navigate my grief. I've always believed that the hymns that have stood the test of time are those that have a heavenly perspective. They draw our minds and hearts away from the daily challenges of life, and reframe our thinking, enabling us to be ready to face the worst that this life or the devil can throw at us; assuring us that we will ultimately be OK. This knowledge, as is attested to in the following journal entries, perhaps contains the ultimate key of how I was able to walk the slow road through the valley of the shadow of death.

1 November 2016

Psalm 100 [says]

Shout for joy to the LORD, all the earth.
Worship the LORD with gladness; come before him with joyful songs.
Know that the LORD is God, It is he who made us, and we are his;
We are his people the sheep of his pasture.
Enter his gates with thanksgiving
and his courts with praise;
give thanks to him and praise his name.

For the LORD is good and his love endures for ever;
his faithfulness continues through all generations.

Andrew Wilson says,

'For those of us who have lived in the light of eternity, Judgement Day will be a day of celebration, not of terror... The plaintiff on the verge of being awarded massive damages does not dread Judgement Day; they can't sleep for excitement, wondering what might be in store.'

'Father, thank you that I am yours, that you made me and that you claim possession of me. Inhabit me fully and lead me completely into your perfect peace.

Father, help me to live in the light of eternity – especially now. Please give me a keener sense of the real reality that exists. May it excite me for my destiny and motivate me in this present reality. In this may I find hope and assurance.'
Amen.

29 November 2016

Ps. 147:10–11. His pleasure is not in the strength of the horse, nor his delight in the legs of a man; the LORD delights in those who fear him, who put their hope in his unfailing love.

I've just finished reading the Psalms. I started reading through Psalms right after Laura died. I remember getting up in the night and reading them aloud – while we were still in George. Having 150 psalms to read has helped me keep in the scripture during this time – and there have been some gems of comfort and help – that I've recorded in this journal.

But I've also seen a contrast between my experience and that of the psalm writers – which I put down to Jesus. Many of the psalms seek for God's punishment to come on enemies... looking for retribution in the face of injustices. Some of what is said seems vindictive and tough to swallow. There's anger expressed – hatred even. This side of Christ I feel that the anger expressed seems incongruent with the Gospel and what Christ did so that all can be saved. Also, [in the New Testament] we learn that our enemy is not flesh and blood – so hatred and anger should be directed differently – and towards the spiritual forces of evil behind human atrocities... and ultimately towards death which takes people into eternal separation from God.

So, although I have perhaps accepted our situation and don't feel bitterness or resentment to God, or anyone, regarding Laura's death, I do want to have God's perspective when it comes to evil, sin, sickness and death... and find motivation to see the Gospel of hope shine brightly in the darkness of evil which is prevalent in the world.

Also, in reading the Psalms, I've noticed again the lack of assurance that the writers have regarding life beyond death. And that makes them cling to life more dearly, seeking justice

> *this side of the grave, and crying out to God for vindication... as well as reward... while here on Earth. The Gospel helps us see in a different dimension... that judgement and reward do come – but not necessarily in the here and now... but ultimately, they come beyond the grave.*

REFLECTION: CHAPTER NINE

Do you find it possible to think of God as hating death, not intending for it to happen? What are your reactions to that?

Tim talks about some difficult emotions – about God 'hating' death and 'jealousy' about Laura's absence from him and presence with her Father. Can you identify any difficult emotions that you have experienced? What do you think is the place of emotions like these in times of unwanted change?

What parts of Tim's journal entries in these pages can you relate to the most? In contrast, what parts don't resonate with you at all? Write/draw/create/do something that expresses your responses.

CHAPTER TEN

STAND FIRM

'His grief he will not forget; but it will not darken his heart, it will teach him wisdom.'

J.R.R. TOLKEIN

22 December 2016

Lonely, but not alone
Silent, screaming with all I am
Tortured, at peace
Broken-hearted, but whole.
Fearful and inadequate
Confused and concerned.
Darkness and light
Shadows in the grey:
Reflections, Memories
The past, the future

> *Though at present*
> *Lonely, but not alone.*

PROJECT MAN

It was sometime just after my brother's wedding in 1996 that he first dubbed me 'Project Man'. I'd had the honour of being his best man and somehow turned this task into an exercise in project management. I felt a sense of responsibility to make sure everything ran smoothly. The ushers and other helpers received lists of what was expected of them. I wanted to be involved in every detail and probably drove people crazy with my micro-management. The nickname adequately describes my love for strategic planning. It is probably a gift – but a gift that can no doubt be irritating to other people who prefer a more chilled-out approach to life.

I guess it was only natural for me to draw on my planning skills when I was assigned this task of surviving through grief. Perhaps I didn't turn it into a 'project' per se, but I did develop a plan and work the plan. That may sound callous. Yet, it was a means of grace to me – utilising my natural inclinations and gifts as a mechanism of survival. I have come to believe that, in the tough times of life, we need to remain true to who God has created us to be. I've mentioned previously that obsessive list-making helped me survive. As did preparing for an overseas trip. Even while we were still in George (which was in August), I felt a strong urge not to spend Christmas in Cape Town. The thought of having to face Christmas in our own home just seemed overwhelming. So, the first real decision I made after Laura's death was that the four of us would head to England for Christmas to be with our British family. I also felt it would provide a good transition point for us, knowing that we'd need to return in January 2017 to face whatever the future looked like – the new abnormal.

Going to the UK seemed like a good idea, but it came with certain realities. The children's passports had all expired (British and South African passports) and so, in order to make that part of the plan work out, there was a huge amount of administration required. However, Project Man faced the challenge and six weeks later had a full-house of five passports – three South African and two British. As Erin is still awaiting British citizenship, I then needed to apply for her visa. But by December, Team Tucker was in the UK for Christmas, and I had the satisfaction of having reached one of my critical goals.

I noted in my journal that my propensity to plan was ultimately a gift of grace that accompanied me along my journey of grief:

> **3 October 2016**
>
> *It dawned on me yesterday that I've been working the plan that formed in the immediate aftermath of our tragedy. This is a gift of God's grace to me – knowing that planning and executing a plan is my key to sanity.*

At times it was exhausting and frustrating and I wished I would allow myself to just vegetate and sulk in self-pity. But that would have been a denial of who God has created me to be. I am Project Man! And it was one thing that helped draw continuity between my old and new normal. Clearly, this is something unique to my disposition. You may be reading this and could think of nothing worse as you face your own challenges. Perhaps the critical question is, how has God wired you? What strengths do you have that you can draw on? I don't believe that we should dumb down our strengths during a time of crisis. Rather, we need to rediscover our purpose, find a sense of continuity... and that means to continue to play to your strengths.

REDEEMING THE PAIN

The seismic shift that Laura's death caused made me question what the future held. I received the wise counsel from a number of people not to make any rash decisions. I thought seriously about moving back to the UK or just selling the house to avoid facing the memories it contained. I considered taking a couple of years off work in order to continue home-schooling the children. Yet, I never felt it right to make any major changes. Some people talked to me about remarriage; asking if I was considering it (one of my close friends insensitively raised the subject within a month of Laura passing – but he's the kind of person who can get away with it! I wouldn't include that in any typical grief-counselling situation). My standard response was that I'd had an incredibly happy marriage to Laura, so I couldn't imagine finding that again. I wasn't interested in thinking too much about the 'happy ever after' story. I decided that I needed to think and plan as if I would be single for a long time. That helped me, initially. And when new love did break into my life, it was an unexpected interruption into my new abnormal that I hadn't been seeking or anticipating. But that's a grace story for another time (and another book).

As I began to think about what the future would look like, there were some foundational principles that helped me face the future I didn't choose. The first was that I wanted to continue to live a life of purpose. I noted this quote from William Wilberforce, the great abolitionist, in my journal:

> 'No one, however, has the right to do nothing. We all have a great eternal work that we are called to accomplish, eternity demands that we use this short and precarious life as well as we can. But aside from that, in a world as needy as ours, surely health and leisure and financial wealth should be able to find some ignorance to instruct, some worry to redress, some want to supply, some mercy to alleviate. Won't ambition and greed ever go to sleep in our hearts? We are so quick to discover new things to desire, so eager to pursue them; why can't we be as hungry to find use in our lives for a Christlike spirit of love?'

With Laura's passing, the gap closed between this finite life, and the promise of heaven. As mentioned in the previous chapter, an eternal perspective motivated me to finding purpose on Earth. Wilberforce expresses it well. I had experienced the precariousness of this life, but that meant that, from now on, I wanted to make every day count. This primarily related to parenting the children. However, this also specifically related to my role with The Message Trust. I wasn't certain I'd be able to continue as CEO. I was facing a decreased capacity for work. As someone who has always had a high output, I contemplated whether I should simply lower my expectations and ask for a different position within the organisation. However, I did know that The Message was more than a job for me. It connected me to my life calling; my passion to see young leaders from the margins have an opportunity to flourish in faith and life. More than that, The Message was a global family. They had rejoiced with me in my successes during the initial pioneering phase of the organisation in South Africa. And they grieved with me when Laura died. The support I received was phenomenal and I don't take it for granted. So, I knew in my heart that I wanted to stay connected to The Message. Now, further down the line, I'm extremely grateful that I did (even remaining as CEO)!

The second principle naturally follows this. I wanted to live in a way that would honour Laura's life. I recorded a summary of what this would mean:

> **3 September 2016**
>
> *Ultimately the best way to honour Laura will include the following:*
>
> - *Investing in the kids as they continue in Christ's love and carry her spirit in all they do.*
> - *Serving the poor – Observatory*
> - *Reaching people with the Gospel*
> - *Worshipping God wholeheartedly*
> - *Africa – serving Africans – creating space for Africans to flourish*
> - *Honour her creativity and hospitality in the home*
> - *Continue to make decisions in faith.*

Sometimes the devastation of a future without Laura hits me – and it just seems so overwhelming. We had so much to look forward to our trip to Kenya, Caleb's first day at high school, Laura transitioning out of home-schooling and wanting to get more involved with The Message, the kids growing and developing in their personalities and gifting, who they would meet and marry – meeting their life partners whom she was praying for, them driving, graduating, getting married – having kids.

And we were looking forward to life after the kids move out of home – all the possibilities that would have opened up to us to do life together, travel, be in ministry, serve across Africa – do whatever crazy stuff God would ask us to do.

I'm not just grieving Laura who has gone, but I'm grieving the wife she was becoming and would become – the future we had planned together. And it's hard to now face the future without her. So hard.

As hard as it seemed, it was a gift of grace to contemplate that her death could have some meaning if it motivated me to serve others and make a difference in the world. This was the seedbed for forming the Laura Tucker Legacy Fund. I'd considered this very early and shared the idea with family and friends at the memorial service. Initially, I simply didn't have the capacity to pursue it. However, in early 2017 I put some flesh to my ideas and founded the fund to help under-privileged South African children in their education. It was a concern close to Laura's heart and we decided that we should initially support children known to the family. The Laura Tucker Legacy Fund partners with a school in Pretoria that she helped found, offering scholarship places to some dear children who are benefitting greatly from the opportunity. Channelling my efforts and including the children in this endeavour has been extremely helpful to me. More information on the fund is contained in the appendix.

Even writing this book has been part of seeking to redeem the pain and draw out something positive from my grief. If my experience can help others face their own tragedy and discover grace in the midst of grief, then my pain has not been in vain.

So, the first principle was that I wanted to continue to live a life of purpose and the second was that I desired to live in a way that honoured Laura. The third principle has been to be unshakeable with regards to my faith.

My eldest son, Caleb, shared the following verse with me a couple of days after the memorial service:

> Where O death is your victory?
> Where O death is your sting?
>
> The sting of death is sin and the power of sin is the law.
> But thanks be to God! He gives us the victory through our Lord Jesus Christ.
>
> Therefore, my brothers and sisters, stand firm, let nothing move you. Always give yourselves fully to the work of the Lord, because you know that your labour in the Lord is not in vain.
>
> 1 CORINTHIANS 15:56-58

This verse became something of a mantra for me as I began to rebuild my life in 2017. I mentioned above that we went to the UK for Christmas at the end of 2016. It was the right decision and enabled us to spend time with loved ones during a very emotional time. However, the day came when we had to board the plane and return to South Africa. It was one of the toughest times of my whole journey. I wrote a little about it in my book on servant leadership, *Grab A Towel*. I took inspiration from the example of one of my biblical heroes, King Hezekiah, who faced his enemies with *steel in his spine*. He unswervingly maintained his confidence in God even when under severe attack. But his courage was contagious and caused confidence to surge among his people. I needed that kind of steel in my spine. I needed to stand firm in the decision that we would face the future, trusting that our faith in God would not be in vain. So, we boarded the plane and departed into the future we didn't choose... the one we continue to live today.

MOVING THROUGH NOT MOVING ON

As we faced 2017, the children starting school, me returning to work full-time, and all the adjustments of our new abnormal, a few people observed that we seemed to be doing well as a family. And we were. But it was tough. The sixth sense still exerted huge influence on me. The two-sided coin of joy and pain caused oscillating emotions. I cried when I dropped the children off at school on the first day. Their bravery overwhelmed me as they faced a life that was beyond recognition to what it had been six months previously. And I had to pinch myself that it had just been six months. I'd lived in slow motion and it felt like years had passed.

As people observed us adjusting, rediscovering purpose and even beginning to flourish – particularly as I entered into a new relationship – some people may have been forgiven for thinking I'd 'moved on'. However, I never saw it that way… I continued to move *through* grief. But the valley of the shadow of death is not a place where we should settle. It's a place we should move through. In mid-2018, I noted this quote from Pete Greig in my journal:

> 'It's a common human tendency to settle in our grief, to redefine the geography of our lives according to the contours of our pain. And of course, when we are bereaved, it's important to stop for a while and lament our loss. It's not healthy to continue as if nothing is wrong. But neither is it helpful to make our disappointment our permanent domain'.

I found this incredibly helpful. God's plan for our family was to be healthy. Yes, I carry scars and there's going to be a lot for the children to work through over the course of their life. The sixth sense is still part of the legacy of all that happened in 2016. I struggle in certain situations and, beyond remarriage, my wife experiences some of the things that can trigger sadness and deep emotions, seemingly out of nowhere. But, ultimately, God wants the kids and me to move through this loss and into the future he has for us. Our sense of loss is not our permanent domain. We didn't 'move on' in the sense of drawing a line that disconnected our future from what we had experienced. Rather, we moved through phases of grief that have influenced and shaped who we are, even as we transition into our new future.

GRACE

This quote from *The Shack* hopefully sums up what you've experienced in reading this book.

> 'Grace doesn't depend on suffering to exist, but when there is suffering you will find grace in many facets and colours.'

In my journey of grief, I have experienced grace in many facets and colours. As I've faced my unchosen future, it has enabled me to drink long and deeply from a fountain of grace that I would not have experienced. That is a comforting thought.

A primary means of grace has been my journal. Like planning, writing is part of how I'm wired. For others it could be singing, poetry, painting, sports activity or some other adventurous pursuit. Again, if you are in the valley, then I advise that you find your medium of grace that can help you rediscover joy. For me, writing is a means of grace. This book has contained snippets and entries from the journal I wrote between 18th August and 24th December 2016. As I've read back over my journal, it has reminded me of the many facets and colours of grace that emerged through suffering.

It is therefore fitting that I close this book with two final journal entries. As the simple black-covered notebook I utilised for my journal was nearly filled up with months of thoughts and notes, I had a sense that God was leading me into a new phase of my grief. The following two entries help capture the nature of how I was sensing and experiencing this. The themes of Grief and Grace are captured in these paragraphs: survival, life in slow motion, the new abnormal, running with a heavy heart and the coexistence of joy and pain. My faith in God as my ally permeates the words and reminds me that he was, and remains, the anchor for my soul.

30 November 2016

Nearing the end of the most intense journal of my life and hopefully I'll never have anything like this again.

And almost 15 weeks on the abnormal is beginning to feel normal – which I could never have imagined. Caleb said he's accepted it. I don't know if I have had an issue of 'accepting' Laura's death... but certainly accepting this new life has been and is a challenge. But Laura always said I'd be OK [if she passed away before me] and although I think of her constantly and miss her intensely – I can learn the secret of contentment even in this. Is that right and appropriate? The reality is that it's still new and fresh although it feels like an eternity. But in some strange way, it feels like God has prepared me for this.

I was in the office for [2017] planning yesterday – and at first it was tough. But as I settled, I almost felt 'back in the saddle' and the team were amazing with their encouragement. I'm reminded of the anointing for leadership – and God's gifts are irrevocable... so I need to learn to operate in that as well – even in this 'new normal' (with that becoming a cliché). I'm also wondering If I draw a bit of a line with this journal coming to an end. It's a sacred document that has helped me find God in this trauma... and has been an invaluable means of grace. And perhaps I need to seal that in some way – and with the next journal, look for God's focus for me for the new season. Not really drawing a line but acknowledging something of a shift... new grace for the new season. Not that I won't reflect or remember Laura or even still weep as I did on Saturday, but just seek to approach things differently... looking beyond this intense period of mourning, remaining grateful, but also having anticipation that God is still at work and he has brought us through this and in to other things that he has planned for us.

24 December 2016

I dreamt about Laura. One of the clearest dreams since she died. I don't know if she was human or an angel in the dream. She was helping me distribute her jewellery to those who wanted to receive specific items. So, she was either already gone in the dream (so it was a dream in the present) – or she was aware she was going to die and was making preparations (a dream in the past).

I prefer the former. The latter reminds me that Laura was robbed of the chance to prepare for death. But, if it was a dream in the present... post-death... it is like she is involved with me in my grief and helping me through this time.

> *Although I know that either way it was just a dream and wasn't really Laura, I do trust God with my dreams and pray that he'll speak to me in all things... at my point of need.*
>
> *And so, this journal concludes – the most tragic period of my life is in record... and writing has certainly helped me to survive. And while I'm still uncertain as to what the future holds, I do know in whose hands I stand... and I continue to trust my faithful God.*

The journey of grief and grace can be confusing and unpredictable. If you are facing a future you didn't choose, I pray that you will also find your hope, strength and peace in God. Psalm 62 became a foundational passage of the Bible for me as I began to rebuild my life. I pray that you will also be able to put your trust in God, pour out your heart to him, and experience him as your rock and refuge.

> Yes, my soul, find rest in God;
> my hope comes from him.
> Truly he is my rock and my salvation;
> he is my fortress, I will not be shaken.
> My salvation and my honour depend on God[a];
> he is my mighty rock, my refuge.
> Trust in him at all times, you people;
> pour out your hearts to him,
> for God is our refuge.
>
> PSALM 62:5-8

REFLECTION: CHAPTER TEN

Tim describes being 'Project Man' as something that provided continuity between the old and new normals. Is there an equivalent of this in your life?

What aspects of your talents, personality, habits and strengths might be continuous for you in a similar way?

Tim describes three principles that became very important in helping him face the future: to live a life of purpose, to honour Laura's life, and to be unshakeable in faith.

Spend a little time thinking about each of them; can you imagine them, or something like them, being similarly foundational for you? How might you put them into practice?

What is your reaction to the idea of 'moving through not moving on'? Is there another way you would express this?

To conclude the reflection guide, we have included a meditation exercise on the next page that you may find helpful.

MEDITATION

A prayerful reflection on Jesus in the Garden of Gethsemane

Take one minute of silence to prepare yourself to be with God, and to listen to what God is saying to you.

Read the accounts of Jesus praying in the Garden of Gethsemane on the night before his death. First, read Matthew 26:36–46, then read Luke 22:39–46. Try to read them slowly, paying attention to the details. Try to picture what is happening; maybe imagine yourself in the Garden with Jesus and the disciples.

What details stick with you?

Do either of Matthew's or Luke's versions resonate more with you? If so, why do you think that is?

How does Jesus deal with his grief here?

What is the new (ab)normal that Jesus is facing? What about the disciples?

What grace does Jesus ask for and receive along with the grief? What about the disciples?

Write, draw, or create something to articulate your response to this scene.

Take one minute of silence to allow what God has been saying and doing to settle in you before you continue with your day.

It may be helpful to repeat this exercise at different stages in your life, and during different experiences. If you do this, try to observe any differences in your experience of it.

EPILOGUE
BY ANDY HAWTHORNE

As I have read this moving and heart-breaking book, my mind has flashed back to that time almost three years ago when I received the news from Tim that Laura had been rushed into hospital and that things really didn't look good. Seven thousand miles away in Manchester we started to pray, and we prayed with faith and anticipation that all would be well. Surely the God who had so clearly led us into Message South Africa wouldn't take the woman who had been so instrumental in making it all happen? We've seen so many miracles over the years and very often God has taken us right to the wire only to come through for us at the very last minute. I felt obviously concerned for my friend Tim but also confident that we were about to get another opportunity to praise the Lord for miraculous breakthrough. It was therefore a complete shock when I got further devastating news from Tim that just a few hours later, Laura had died.

As I sat in bed with my wife Michele and we started to process what we had heard, I felt confused and frustrated. I know we all have to die sometime and felt comfort in the fact that Laura was enjoying what the Bible calls 'eternal pleasures at his right hand' but I also felt frustrated. She was quite simply a beautiful soul with so much to offer the world this side of heaven. She was 38 years old and a mother of three, for Pete's sake! She was our friend and co-worker and she was absolutely my friend's soulmate. It all felt so wrong.

So much has happened in the last three years as God has, in the way only he can, started to redeem this tragic situation. One of the greatest and most encouraging things in my life and ministry is to see Tim now firing on all cylinders again after being so worried for him in those devastating early days but of course we are all left with questions, some of which will only be answered on the final day.

Questions down here like 'how could any good come out of this' started to be answered within a few days as we shared in the most moving memorial service imaginable in Cape Town. I'm sure you will be challenged as you read the tribute to Laura from that service at the back of this book. If you are, all I can say is 'you should have been there!' There was a tangible sense of God's presence as the family shared their grief but also challenged us all to seize the day and love those around us. It's also been answered over the last months as we have watched and been inspired by Tim's 'grown-up Christianity'. Not once has he doubted or cursed the Lord and out of it has come this inspiring book that I am sure will be a help and comfort to so many.

One thing's for sure, all of us will know that most intense and deep human experience of grief at some time or other but reading stories like this can help us to know that we can come out at the other side fighting and also know that maybe occasionally, clinging on by our fingernails, we will be given strength to say 'the Lord gives, the Lord takes away, blessed be the name of the Lord' (Job 1:21).

THE LAURA TUCKER LEGACY FUND

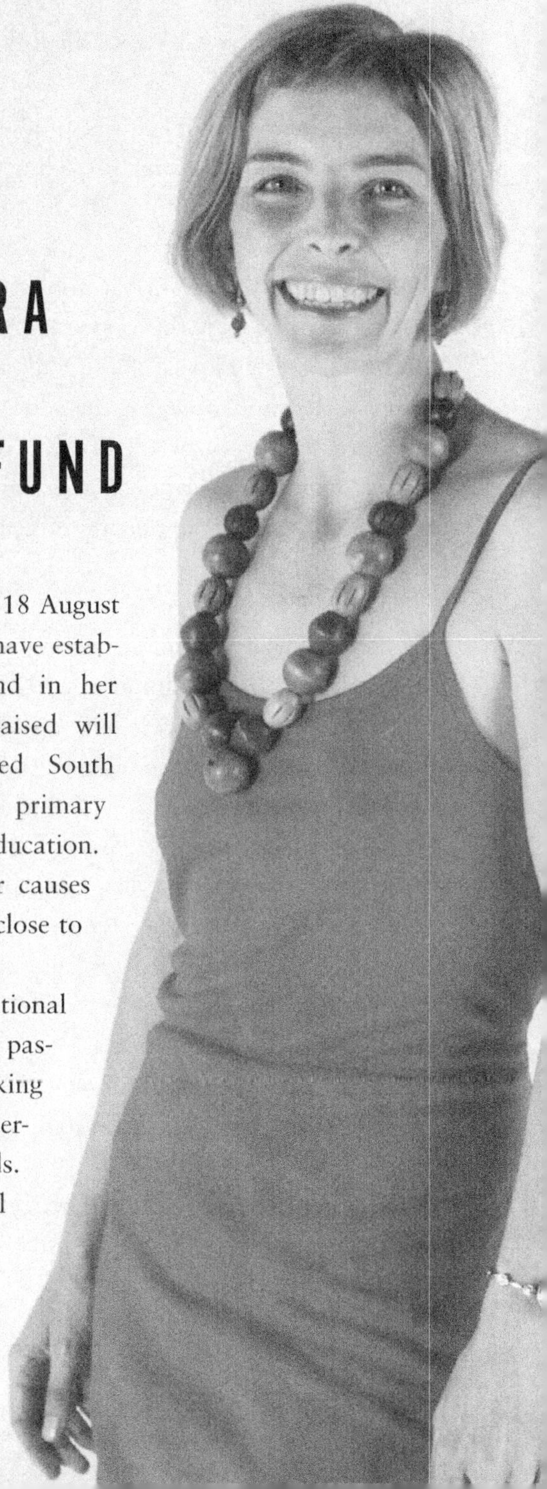

Laura passed away on 18 August 2016. As a family, we have established this legacy fund in her memory. The funds raised will support underprivileged South African children from primary through to tertiary education. We also support other causes that would have been close to Laura's heart.

As an Occupational Therapist, Laura was passionate about working with children from underprivileged backgrounds. She also saw how vital education was in helping children out of poverty and to fulfil their potential in life. The fund will be a way of continuing Laura's legacy through providing financial grants to assist with school fees and other schooling costs.

The proceeds of Grief and Grace will be allocated to the legacy fund. Any additional donations will enable the fund to grow and provide this opportunity to more children in the future. Representatives of the Simpson and Tucker families allocate the funds towards the education of children that fit the criteria laid out by the family. Tim and Laura's children, Caleb, Samuel and Erin, will also be involved in this process.

Thank you for supporting the legacy fund through purchasing this book.

The family will keep all contributors aware of the progress of the beneficiary children through an annual update. The fund is being freely administered by partner charities in the US, UK and South Africa to enable tax-deductible donations to be made. All the money raised will go directly to the beneficiaries!

It is the hope of the Simpson and Tucker families that this fund will be a way that many people around the world will be able to remember Laura in a way that honours the amazing woman that she was, and also continues her legacy in a way that would make her smile!

With our love and gratitude,
The Tucker and Simpson families

Please email us at **lauratuckerlegacy@gmail.com** to find out how you can support the fund and continue Laura's legacy.

THE LAURA TUCKER LEGACY FUND

If you have found this book helpful, then please also consider paying it forward and making a donation so that we can provide the book freely to others who may benefit.

For more information, please see the website:

GRIEFANDGRACE.ORG

MEMORIAL SERVICE TRIBUTE

I met Laura within 24 hours of landing in South Africa on my first trip here in 1998. We were having a movie night at a friend of my cousin's (now a friend of mine... he still says I owe him)! Laura was there... and my first impression was of her jaw-dropping beauty! We chatted during that evening – apparently her first impression of me was that she couldn't understand my Manchester accent and that she had never met anyone so pale!

But from that moment – until our final perfect day together on Earth, a week last Tuesday – which we spent on the beach at Victoria Bay with our children and my brother's family... she has made my life more beautiful and my world more colourful... (and my accent has changed considerably as well)!

The support we've received since Laura's death has been phenomenal... and I want to express our heartfelt thanks.

Firstly to Laura's parents. Your daughter loved you so much and I want to thank you for your role in making her the incredible person that she was.

To the broader family. Having you all at George last weekend was testimony to the bond we share – not just as family… but in our faith. We share in this deep grief… but we also share in the tremendous hope in Christ. Also to Mark, Alastair and Danielle who came to weep with and support all of us.

To Andy and Michele and all at The Message. These past three years being in Cape Town and part of The Message were a tremendous blessing to Laura. The mission of The Message was right at the heart of Laura's passion for the poor… and for Africa. In particular – we found great joy in working together on initiating the first Eden team right here with Jubilee in Salt River.

To our Jubilee family. Although we haven't been here long… Laura felt so at home here since we moved from Cape Town. And also to our church families in Pretoria – Eastside Community Church and in the UK at Mottram Evangelical Church. Our family has felt your love and support over many years… in the good times and the difficult times.

I want to thank those who have travelled a long way to be here today… and also to everyone who has sent messages of support. We have been overwhelmed by your love and practical help during these difficult days.

To Caleb, Sammy and Erin. Our children – Mommy loved you very much and you were the apple of her eye. She was so proud of each one of you and loved being your mommy more than anything else.

And to the LORD. I can't imagine going through this without the strength of our faith that God is in control and that it will not be long until we're reunited with Laura again.

I asked the children to each share a special memory of their Mom that they cherish… and also to let you know how they are feeling.

Erin remembers Laura taking her to get her hair done – a monthly challenge… Initially Laura was determined to braid Erin's hair herself… but then started taking her to the salon – an ordeal that could last up to four hours with Erin screaming at the top of her voice 'I want my daddy'. Laura would cry with Erin as she endured the pain… but the end result was always worth it as Erin looks so gorgeous! When we got back from George, Erin drew a picture of Laura in heaven – dancing with God. Erin feels that Mom is OK and enjoying heaven. She says that everything will be OK.

Samuel remembers playing table tennis with Mommy in the garden. This is a special memory because Laura saw a table-tennis table being put out on the side of the road as a family no longer wanted it. The table was a bit beaten up – but typical Laura, she made a plan. I had to get the work bakkie,[5] pick up the table… and with a bit of TLC – we had our own table-tennis table in the garden. Just one bargain to add to the many she chalked up over the years (and Sammy is turning into a fine table tennis player). Samuel has a verse which has helped him since he heard that Laura was critically ill… it's Romans 8:28 'And we know that in all things God

5 South African term for a pickup truck.

works for the good of those who love him, who have been called according to his purpose'.

Caleb's favourite memories are of our times on the beach. Laura loved going to the beach and was never more happy than when the five of us were playing, swimming, rock-pooling, surfing, walking along or just relaxing at the beach. Caleb feels that 'Team Tucker' worked well as five people… and feels that four is an unwholesome number… but says that with God helping us, we will find our new normal.

And me? We've been reading *The Lord of the Rings* as a family and sometimes I wish I was Bilbo Baggins and could use a ring to vanish and not face this. But I'm not going to vanish… we're going to face this and together we'll ultimately be OK. We know that Laura is not dead – as someone told me… she's just changed address, and she's more alive than ever… without pain and waiting for us to join her.

We will make it through this time because we have one another, we have all the people who have been supporting us… and we have the Lord. And so, we say, even as we grieve deeply for the loss of Laura and we don't have all the answers… it is well with my soul. The Lord gives, the Lord takes away, the name of the LORD be praised!

As a family we want you to know that we are praying for all of you… that good will come out of this tragedy. Our heart is that you will be able to take stock, recognising that life is fragile and none of us knows what tomorrow will bring… so make the most of today. Ensure that you are in a right relationship with God through Jesus Christ. Seek reconciliation with those you have offended or have offended you. Strengthen your marriages. Appreciate your children. Serve the poor and share God's love with others. Our time is short – but… as Laura's life is a witness to… our impact can be huge.

I'll close with one of her favourite verses which she would be praying for all of us today:

> Do not be anxious about anything, but in every situation, by prayer and petition, with thanksgiving, present your requests to God. And the peace of God, which transcends all understanding, will guard your hearts and your minds in Christ Jesus.
>
> PHILIPPIANS 4:6–7

ACKNOWLEDGEMENTS

I want to express my warmest gratitude and appreciation to the following people who have helped in the production of this book.

David Tucker: for proof-reading, encouragement and providing great feedback and input.

David Fraser: the best of men! For your support and continued friendship.

Christina Tucker: thanks for the late nights of listening to the early draft and for your love and support every day.

Sincere thanks to the following people who read the manuscript. Through your feedback I received the courage necessary to continue with publishing this book: Gareth Lloyd-Jones, Andy Hawthorne, Janet Greener, Theo Roman, Dalene Reyburn, Dayne Myles and Danielle Campsall.

Thanks to Simon Baker from Thirteen Creative who has weaved his magic over the material and beautifully crafted the end product.

My PA, Annalise Petersen, for your hard work and commitment (and still managing to smile through it all).

And to everyone in The Message Trust around the world. I love being part of this incredible family.